Data Diplomacy

Keeping Peace and Avoiding

Data Governance Bureaucracy

Håkan Edvinsson

Technics Publications

Published by:

2 Lindsley Road, Basking Ridge, NJ 07920 USA
https://www.TechnicsPub.com

Edited by Laura Sebastian-Coleman
Cover design by Lorena Molinari
Cover photo by Li Fernstedt

First Printing 2020
Copyright © 2020 by Håkan Edvinsson

ISBN, print ed.   9781634626767
ISBN, Kindle ed.   9781634626774
ISBN, ePub ed.   9781634626781
ISBN, PDF ed.   9781634626798

Library of Congress Control Number: 2019951991

Contents

Foreword

It is exciting to have had a small part in the making of this book, which presents a fresh set of insights about the work involved in information architecture and data governance and, with these insights, the potential for organizations to get more value from their data. I first met Håkan Edvinsson in 2016 via email. At the time, I was editing the DMBOK2 and he was the primary contributor on the Data Architecture chapter. The first time I sent him an edited version of his chapter, he thanked me and then suggested that we should talk. He lives in Sweden and I live in Connecticut. Fortunately, we both live in the twenty-first century, and could connect electronically. We Skyped several times before the work was finished.

Two things struck me about these conversations. First, the energy and intelligence that Håkan brought to the discussion on data architecture. He was not, as some architects can be, simply in love with his own work. Instead he was interested in the kinds of problems that architecture could solve. And he understood why architecture is important: because without a thoughtful approach to data architecture, we will not be able to tap into the potential value of data. But with a thoughtful approach, we can see additional opportunities to use and generate value through data. He provided interesting examples, from the automobile industry to the cleaning business, to illustrate his ideas and clarify his points.

The second thing that struck me was the caliber of our discussions about the text of his chapter. By the time I sent Håkan his chapter, it had been through public commentary, an initial edit, and my editing. I tend to edit with a very heavy hand. Sometimes I may cut a little deep in pursuit of clarity. This was, I think, Håkan's impression during our first email exchange. "I don't recognize this as my text," he said. So, we started talking it through. Both of us asked questions. Both of us listened. Though we did not discuss it explicitly, I think both of us recognized we were dependent on each other to meet our common goal: a clear, accurate, and informative chapter, one that he could be proud of as primary contributor, and one that I knew worked cohesively within the DMBOK2. We negotiated and collaborated until both of us were satisfied with the outcome. In the end, we got to a better place together than either one of us would have gotten to alone. And I got my first taste of Håkan's diplomatic skills.

Håkan and I met in person at the Enterprise Data World (EDW) Conference in 2018. At this point, the DMBOK2 had been out for a year. Håkan presented, as he describes in his foreword, on the idea of non-coercive data governance. He introduced himself as a Swede and reminded the audience of the benefits of living in that peaceful democracy. He drew on the work of Daniel Kahneman, author of Thinking Fast and Slow, to show that we sometimes misunderstand our own reactions and misread the actions of others. Then he shared a set of stories that illustrated how we can get better results and more buy-in for data governance if we are not only self-aware but also aware of what other stakeholders actually have at stake in their interactions around data.

After the presentation, I felt like I had finally heard some new ideas about data governance. This was the same conference at which people were claiming that "Data Governance is dead." But Håkan had described how it could be alive and well, if practiced in a different way. Following the conference, we exchanged email about the concept of Data Diplomacy – a different way of thinking about the role of information architecture in data management, the challenges of data governance, and even about data itself. Now he has fully fleshed out his ideas and introduced a new concept that I think will be of great use to any organization trying to improve its overall approach to data management.

Laura Sebastian-Coleman, Ph.D., CDMP

Author: *Measuring Data Quality for Ongoing Improvement.*
Navigating the Labyrinth: An Executive Guide to Data Management.

Production Editor: *DAMA Data Management Body of Knowledge (DMBOK2), Second Edition.*

Acknowledgments

I owe a great deal to Laura Sebastian-Coleman, for coming up with the initial idea for this book, for encouraging me to take the project on and for supporting me throughout the writing. I also thank my wife and family for their moral support and their practical help. Thank you, Hazel Clarke and Mark Barringer for helping me to express myself in a foreign language.

Whenever there is a quote, it is that person's true words. Wherever I have been inspired by someone, and I am aware of it, it has been noted. Everywhere else it is simply based on my true experience. It is possible that I could just have been inspired unknowingly by someone and have simply forgotten the origin of an idea. If that has happened in this book, I am truly sorry for not mentioning that person.

I cannot write about running data governance in a large organization without mentioning Robert S. Seiner, the inventor of the "non-invasive data governance"[1] concept. I have adopted very much of his approach to establish data governance. My intention is to take this a step further by adding a non-coercive concept and diplomatic data governance behavior.

---

[1] *Non-Invasive Data Governance: The Path of Least Resistance and Greatest Success*, by Robert S. Seiner. Technics Publications 2014.

As I do not have a completely comprehensive knowledge of this topic, I have invited a group of people to discuss data diplomacy as they have many insights in these matters. I wish to thank the following for their invaluable assistance, experience and contributions. This writing process could not have come into fruition without these knowledgeable contributors.

Lena Lindroth, Jonny Salo-Premmert, Joachim Bondeson, Ove Sirefeldt, Mimmi Nilsson, Johan Lindholm, Sofie Fischer, Michael Åsman, Pelle Graveleij and Jenny Lundholm.

Data diplomacy disclaimer:

There is an alternative meaning of the data diplomacy notion with a political and social perspective which is about being able to share data for the public good all over the world. It may, for example, include the sharing of big data sources within drug research, epidemics and medical care. Such variant of data diplomacy is handled deeper in other literature rather than here.

Introduction

When I gave a speech at the international 2018 Enterprise Data World (EDW) conference, I opened by mentioning a few personal facts about myself combined with a short description of the country I come from: Sweden. I usually do this at international conferences instead of talking about my profession and the organization I represent. Not only does this avert any confusion between my country and Switzerland, but also it demystifies what type of foreign country I have traveled from. I find that this develops a better relationship between myself and the audience.

The speech at EDW was about various data governance challenges, especially how to gain managerial interest for the topic. What I did not understand, until Laura Sebastian-Coleman mentioned it to me afterwards, was that the way I depicted Sweden influenced the conception of my entire speech. The messages I put across delivered a slightly different twist than I had originally intended.

The peaceful democratic kingdom of Sweden has witnessed peace since 1814, that is, for more than 200 years. This country in Northern Europe has managed to stay out of two world wars, even with waring activities literal on its doorstep. That could not have happened without diplomacy and flexibility. Furthermore, the country has a history of taking diplomatic roles in the United Nations and has acted as an intermediate negotiator in some notable international settlements. So, there must be some natural behaviors and mindsets for finding diplomatic solutions here, rather than solving disagreements with violence. Despite being a small non-violent country of just 10 million citizens, we have our share of innovations, startups and a growth of large multinational industries. Today, companies like IKEA, H&M, Ericsson and Volvo, and innovations like Spotify, Skype and Candy Crush Saga are known all over the world. Mentioning this is not for the sake of bragging; but merely to put forward the idea that there are no contradictions between success and diplomacy.

My speech at EDW was about the benefit of having a non-coercive approach in data management in general, and, particularly in data governance. The reception my speech gained was somewhat biased by my opening with the statement of 200 years of peace in Sweden. I was unaware of this at the time, but it had set a precedent for the messages, improved the trustworthiness, and, it had mind-primed the audience of what is possible. As a result, the idea to set all this out in a book evolved.

I started with looking back a few decades and contemplating what the common denominators of the data governance establishments are and why they have been successful. For instance, where the data governance work implemented changes which brought value to its stakeholders, being recognized and requested, and implied a durable change toward the mindset that data as such is indeed valuable. The conclusion was that working with purposes, trusts, behavior and willingness to implement win-win solutions is far more important than the data governance formalities. Thus, applying some of core aspects of diplomacy to data governance is probably an understandable explanation to a well-integrated and benefitable data governance. It made sense.

I saw my first data model while studying at the university back in 1985. I stared at it and did not get it. I have never forgotten that first time. It was not self-explanatory, which is an important lesson for all data architects. As I started working with it in my first job it quickly became my favorite tool and a natural part for model-driven business improvements and requirements.

This was during the fourth-generation programming language (4GL) years, which were very data modeling intense times. A group of guys at the IT department at the Swedish national airline company had developed a method for doing data modeling with business representatives in workshops. They started a consultancy agency where I spent 15 years. Here I practiced the ability to spread the doctrine of data as a resource and to work with the development of data with, and inside, the business.

During these years, I worked with these issues in virtually all industries and different kinds of companies. I became the senior training manager of a data architecture certification program which after a few years became an enterprise architecture program. At this time, most of the books about data modeling were written from the data modeler's and the data architect's viewpoint, focusing on the modeling theories and various modeling situations. I lacked a handbook to describe how to design, establish and live with a data-driven enterprise architecture, the main messages I was teaching in the certification program. So, I wrote one together with a colleague[2]. That book took me to the DAMA project working on the second edition of Data Management Body of Knowledge[3], by writing the Data Architecture chapter and a few other topics which were included in other chapters.

So, what do I want to accomplish with this book? The attempt with this book is to define the data diplomacy approach and to describe the data diplomacy behavior related to data. It is a compilation mostly of my own experiences and what I have picked up from people I have met or worked with. I think everybody should share their experiences. Especially those where things have really turned out well.

---

[2] *Enterprise Architecture Made Simple*, Edvinsson & Aderinne, Technics Publications 2013.

[3] *DAMA Data Management Body of Knowledge*, Technics Publications 2017.

This is not a novel. There is no butler who did it and no one will be married in the end. However, hopefully there is peace, hope, future and a treasure somewhere, without suggesting this is a fairy tale. The book is preferably read from to start to finish to get the gist of the data diplomacy concept, as the ingredients of it are introduced in steps. But it is fine to dip into anything that seems interesting; as you would be reading a book of poems or proverbs, not that I suggest this book is art.

As a reader, some awareness of the challenges of managing data is preferred and useful, but not critical. A few concepts within the data management topic are frequently used and good to be aware of.

- *Data governance* – the exercise of authority and control over the management of data assets[4] to ensure that data is managed properly, improved when needed and properly designed for the benefits of the organization and its stakeholders.

- *Data model* – documentation of a data structure consisting of vital business concepts, referred as 'entities', enriched with definitions, attributes, relationships and business rules.

---

[4] *DAMA The Data Management Body of Knowledge*, Technics Publications 2017.

- *Data architect* – a person with the capability to design how data should be organized, stored, processed and transferred.

This book is primarily intended for CIO's, CDO's, chief architects, data strategists, data governance leads and data architects. It is for anyone who is struggling with data quality, data accountability, and the concept of data as a valuable asset. It is for those who seek for the next generation of data governance, when the first generation was riddled by formality or just did not take off. The book is written as a dialog from me and those who are in the frontline of the quest for data improvement. It is organized in four parts.

- The first chapter introduces the concept of data diplomacy and illustrates it through a set of real-life cases where diplomacy played a crucial part.

- The second chapter introduces four arenas for performing diplomatic data governance and describes the activities that go on in each of the arenas.

- The third chapter details the four data governance arenas including the minimum set of roles that are needed when instituting data governance using a diplomatic approach.

- The fourth chapter is a toolbox for the data diplomat, that contains various methodology hints.

CHAPTER 1

The concept of Data Diplomacy

There is much to discuss concerning this topic, such as why we should use diplomacy in data management and especially within data governance and data design. Also what this means in practice, for whom and how we can accomplish a diplomatic workspace. Below is a brief introduction to data diplomacy, including a few real-world examples.

Why do we need diplomacy in data governance?

The expectations on data governance are high: if we fix the data, we will have fewer problems in our organization and we will be able to make better decisions. The business value from that is obvious. Having the data accurate, available and understandable is of course important and efficient in any kind of work. Typically, data governance strives to:

- secure the business data quality and security

- unify business semantics,

- clarify decision-making, accountabilities and quality specifications for business data.

Drivers for data governance include regulatory reasons, quality cost drivers or the need to innovate. In order to be successful, data governance must impact several layers in the organization:

- Managerial – data governance must align to or influence accountabilities and responsibilities, on resolution of concerns, and on how the business is monitored.

- Operational – data governance has an impact on the details of the day-to-day operations to ensure data correctness, security and availability.

- Changes – data governance must be a part of changed work, regarding processes and IT, in order to ensure that new or changed systems mean improvements also for the data governance goals.

Data governance is commonly organized on top of, or parallel with, the formal organization structure. It may need to coexist with a business process management structure, combined with a world-wide geographical range and with cultural differences among various professions. Of course, high expectations and complexity pose many challenges.

After over a decade of efforts to implement effective data governance, there are those who begin to question whether their data governance efforts, including all these roles and standardization activities, will ever meet these expectations. When concepts like "data governance 2.0" come up, we admit that there was something wrong with the first attempt.

A data governance framework consists of roles, responsibilities and procedures. But it does not however tell us how to act when settling conflicts and issues regarding data. Furthermore, these frameworks do not tell us how to prevent data issues from appearing in the first place. When data governance fails there is probably no need for more governance. There is a need for different behavior.

The data diplomacy approach aims to simplify data governance and evolve the behavior regarding data. This enables data governance to deliver value and prevents it from ending up in pointless bureaucracy.

Everybody is a data worker

Everything that is going on in the organization has a piece of data in it; everybody who is performing some kind of physical work is also, as they work, using and producing data. Data is required to perform the work and do the right thing when digging, assembling, cooking, moving, giving medicine, or repairing. Moreover, the data being produced while doing these activities is vital for other purposes such as invoicing, quality innovation, assurance and improving the work, regardless of whether that data is captured, or, remains as tacit knowledge with the person performing the work.

As an example, I saw an excavator that was both digging and laying fiber cable in residential areas. The driver had a map on a flat screen showing where the fiber cable was planned to be laid.

The driver of course encountered some physical obstacles, like stones and trees, that had to be overcome. To capture such deviations from the map, the excavator was equipped with an GPS receiver and while digging, the map was updated to show where the cable would finally end up. Thus, the data was created and recorded in real time, closest to its natural source. And, the driver was both a data worker and a driver.

When it comes to those whose work is intangible, their work is in fact 100% data and knowledge. They can be selling, ordering, communicating, documenting, negotiating, analyzing, organizing or training. For these kinds of work, knowledge and data are everything. They are, in fact, data managers occupied with capturing, storing and sharing data.

What does diplomacy mean in data governance?

Diplomacy means that data governance should not be regarded as a separate thing. Today, when everybody is a knowledge worker, information worker and data worker, governing and managing data is what everybody is already doing. Let's keep this where it already is and should be.

Data governance is not a separate thing, it is just a piece of the ordinary work, or an aspect of it.

Furthermore, data governance is not just about correcting errors. Having data governance for the purpose of fixing bad data is to brand it as reactive and boring work. It would be like keeping to a speed limit and losing weight.

Focusing on data errors is to give data governance a very low ambition; it would imply moving from "bad" to "not bad".

Very few organizations in a competitive market have "not bad" as an ambition to meet a customer's expectations. Instead, data governance could be an enabler for making bold changes right from the start. Acting in the arenas where the important changes take place enables data governance to become valuable.

Data governance is also about the design of the business data we do not yet have.

This leads to another important statement: designing the business' data is a part of designing the business.

Business data design cannot be solely a task of data architects.

Too often IT professionals ask questions to business representatives and then produce a detailed system design based on what the IT person perceives. This is nothing but indirect business design on a second tier of assumptions and opinions. It can almost be regarded as a violation to delegate to IT how the business should be designed. Unfortunately, this happens a lot.

Instead, having representatives from the business responsible for what data should look like, including where and how it is captured, will get things right from start. It will also solve the accountability challenge of data. If businesspeople participate in creating data, they will have a sense of ownership of that data.

This is also bridging business with IT as they will talk about business data – possibly the most important ingredient in both business and IT. Remember what the "I" in "IT" stands for? (Don't worry, we will still need data architects when forming IT solutions.)

Traditional data governance is designed to avoid errors and to resolve issues by escalating them. Data diplomacy adds engagement, cooperation and inclusion to data governance work. With diplomacy, disagreements are resolved using negotiations. Escalating issues ends up with a winner and a loser, whereas diplomacy strives for two winners.

The diplomacy approach strives to reduce the formalities and omit the coercive parts of traditional data governance.

Some governance structures and formalities are of course needed for governing any of the organization's assets, even the data assets. But to reach data harmony, with lasting peace in the organization and the desired behavior, we need diplomacy.

Establishing data governance using a diplomatic approach, is done in a non-invasive and non-coercive way. This means being of service in business improvements wherever it is needed, in the easiest possible way. It also means acknowledging the silent data governance that is already going on.

The diplomacy approach aims for a lean data governance organization with a "just enough" size.

This means having a just few data governance roles, a few decision bodies and a few procedures. It also means that it is implemented only where it is needed. Hence, it keeps things simple and relevant.

So, diplomacy in data governance is about addressing behaviors and planting it to the contexts it is needed.

It is not about doing more. It is about doing things a little bit differently.

Who is a data diplomat?

Data diplomacy is an approach, a way of working, an ambition, a mindset, a movement and eventually, a culture. It is however not a title.

You can act as a data diplomat and work at the sharp end of the operations and managing data as your profession. Or, you can have a managerial position. Or, you can be the head of data governance and be accountable for establishing or rolling out a data governance initiative. Or, you can be a designer of a data governance organization or a framework for it. Or, you can be a data modeler striving to understand, capture or design business data. Or, you can be a data scientist who wants to get hold of and understand large portions of data. You can be an employee or a consultant within the organization.

This means you are someone with a quest for

- improving the data quality, such as accuracy, completeness and correctness,

- improving how we work with data, such as how the data flows and is processed in the value streams the organization takes part in, or,

- improving the work, how we design and build capabilities to process the data in our computers.

So, you are most likely trying to improve how data improvement is done by constantly trying to influence other people with the importance of getting things right with the data. Diplomacy in data governance is about addressing behaviors and putting the right level of data governance in place where it is needed.

How is this done?

So, what is the secret to being successful with data governance using a diplomatic approach? Below is a set of major prerequisites briefly mentioned as teasers. All of them will be further explained in separate sections.

Diplomatic instead of coercive data governance requires just a simple and lean data governance framework.

We do not need an ambitious and complex data governance framework if we focus on behavior. A lean and simple framework is described later, referred to as the "four data governance arenas".

Data governance is based on a set of principles.

Principles will reduce the number of roles and procedures and thus the data governance complexity. Processes, procedures and other formalities force activities to be carried out in determined sequences. Typically, such "linear processes" include steps with checkpoints to assure completeness, accuracy and other quality check-ups. There are of course some occasions when these are needed but for most cases they do usually not fit into reality.

Basing data governance on principles will take trust. Trust, in turn, takes unity of purpose; if we know why we are at work and we strive for common goals, we can trust each other. If the goals are unclear, and incentives are disparate, this will be harder. Experiences show that it is somewhat easier to adopt the diplomatic approach for organizations whose employees are aware of and committed to fulfill the organization's expectations.

The truth is in the data.

Deploying the "the truth is in the data" paradigm means always having the eye on the ball in data governance. It means always looking at the data as it really is instead of making assumptions or guesses. Use the real data in hard discussions as data represents facts and facts are neutral. By looking at actual data, or constructed examples if you do not yet have the data, we can undoubtedly see what it is, how it is connected to other data, what it represents, how it should be organized, where it naturally originates from, its business value, and so on. And, we can immediately see what needs to be improved. Too many discussions are about data semantics, data models, systems contents and systems capabilities, data carriers, and, who should (or should not) do what. These things can quickly become theoretical and emotional. Firstly, it is about the data. Secondly, it is about the rest.

As an IT professional, you work with the business, not toward it, and nor on its behalf unless asked to.

Working *with* the business means working together with business representatives, as opposed to doing it for them and designing business data based on the opinions of data architects. The evolved responsibility of the data architect role is a returning matter in this book.

Acting in a diplomatic way

So, how do we recognize a person that has entered a data diplomacy mode?

First, that person stays neutral in data management matters and constantly sticks to a neutral ground. A diplomat is expected to be neutral. When a conflict of interest appears, or a possible conflict, the diplomat is neutral to both sides. Otherwise, the diplomat becomes the advocate from somebody's standpoint. The data diplomat is rather the advocate of the data from an organizational entirety perspective; for the greater good. You will hear this person remark "the truth is in the data".

A way to keep the neutrality is to be clear when facts are underpinning the diplomat's own standpoint, and, when he or she is merely expressing an opinion. This means in turn that a diplomat is well prepared with facts prior to all important meetings.

A starting point for a diplomat is "I don't know" since this person questions what she or he already knows. You will therefore hear more questions than answers from such a person. A prejudiced person is never diplomatic.

A diplomatic person is frank. Achieving diplomacy on a larger scale, meaning more than just a few individuals, will take trust. And a diplomat, who asks many questions and consistently expects sincere answers, must be trustworthy.

Being diplomatic is to be able to put oneself in another's shoes. This means having empathy for that person's situations, challenges, drives and strives. It means curiosity and learning about what people do and why they do it. Being diplomatic is however not equivalent to being submissive with tiptoeing around the clamorous ones. This person can very well have a strong voice and maintain discipline during workshops and meetings.

A diplomatic person does however not lose her or his temper. This person will not get upset. Anyone who loses their temper in an argument becomes a loser. It is just a job anyway and nothing to get upset about.

If you ask a diplomatic person a question that forces that person to choose sides you will probably either get no answer, or, you will have a suggestion. The diplomat needs to take care of his personal integrity to retain the reputation of diplomacy. Such reputation is a personal brand and takes time to achieve.

Of course, no person can go through life as a fully-fledged diplomat, as depicted above. It could not be possible to live that way, nor to live or work with such a person. Rather, this is about the ability to enter into a diplomatic mode when needed.

Examples of diplomatic behavior

Rather than describing data diplomacy theoretically and comprehensively and how it manifests itself in data management, I prefer to use a few real-life cases to demonstrate the diplomatic behavior I have witnessed or taken part in over the years.

Data governance propulsion using gravity

A recent example of using diplomacy in data governance is Volvo Penta, a brand and a business area within the Volvo Group. They offer power solutions for various marine and industrial applications. They are known for their reliable engines and competent automated maneuvering systems.

Their data governance maturity is outstanding within the Volvo Group and meets very high international standards. Data governance is appreciated and respected within the company, and, it is considered as a valuable part when taking on the company's challenges. This story has been presented at international DAMA conferences.

In 2011 Volvo Penta started managing the business data in a more structured and dedicated way. The main driver for this was quite simple.

We can do better than this.

Hence, it is a business-driven data governance, such as being able to form and implement changes faster, making bold business and product improvements feasible, and improving the business' performances. The data governance work was not driven by regulations or any other external influencing factor. At least not as the driver to initiate data governance work.

The success for Volvo Penta's data governance would not have come to reality without the following ingredients:

- A CIO who paved the way for data governance and made sure the way stays paved.

- A dedicated full-time data governance lead with a vast network and hearty endurance.

- A business-friendly data design graphic and methodology that enabled a wide engagement among business representatives.

Jonny, the CIO, convinced the senior management to delegate important data matters to a couple of data governance councils. Data matters were to be settled by business specialists, rather than having them resolved by IT specialists. Furthermore, he convinced the middle management to permit some of the knowledgeable employees to participate. And, he made sure that data governance was given the opportunity to act whenever and wherever it was needed.

Lena, the data governance lead, was, and still is, informing, teaching, convincing and encouraging people everywhere in the company to take on data challenges. This quest is carried out with an impressive endurance. She has a vast network and long experience with the company, having had lots of different positions and functions over the years. She has a way of detecting where data governance can be of service and is excellent in identifying who to engage.

> "Every week I do one or two Data Governance Introductions. I invite, well, almost demand that, every new person I encounter to be introduced to how we do things here. This includes anyone taking part in a business data design activity, or those who will be part of an IT-solution project, or a new consultant. Initially, I used to do this presentation on a yearly basis to a large group. Today, I want to have not more than four persons at the time, at the most, just to ensure that I convey the messages to every single person and make space for anyone to discuss and ask questions. During this introduction, I explain why we have data governance, how we do it, what we have done, what we expect from everybody and what they can find in our resource libraries."
>
> *Lena Lindroth, Volvo Penta Data Governance Lead*

Beyond these two central characters, there is a pragmatic, non-invasive and diplomatic way of working. They are using simple modeling graphics, they are producing understandable diagrams and diagram descriptions, and they use a working method that has made the business representatives embrace the modeling outcomes. That way, the data design is bridged between business and IT, which facilitates communicating intangible data structures. The way they worked with modeling, and still do, is coherent with what is described later in this book.

"I don't believe in doing data improvement work as a separate initiative in its own right. It needs gravity."

Jonny Salo-Premmert, Volvo Penta CIO

"Gravity" means that something is moving in the organization. Something is rocking the building with enough energy to get people's attention. An example of heavy gravity is the movement from fossil fuels to electric. For a company that has been making engines since 1915, the development toward electric propulsion is huge gravity.

When you can feel the gravity, the executive managers in that movement do not want to be left behind. People become motivated to participate and invest in their resources and personal brand to ensure they have influence on outcome from the movement. Not all movements are that dramatic, though. There are movements with less energy in the gravity, such as new regulations to comply to, or, a need for a new Customer Relationship Management (CRM) system.

Jonny's and Lena's ability to recognize when there is gravity, or not, is a success factor for betting on the right horses; it makes audacious challenges feasible.

Data governance is taking part and contributing where the senior management is pointing their flashlights.

The Volvo Penta data governance program has been implemented in steps; starting with product master data, continuing with customer master data and extending the scope from there. They started with data definitions and designing preferable data structures and continued with the data content. At first, the data governance councils made decisions regarding data structures, relationships, names and definitions, that is, making business data design decisions. When maturing, they started to decide upon common reference data values. After that, they settled how to manage data content in databases.

It took three to four years before the value from data governance became obvious. At that time things were getting more consistent. The customers could detect that data was integrated and easier to retrieve. New improvement projects had reduced risks as the data was connected and well documented. IT projects were starting to finish faster. So, things changed; the data governance went from needing pavement to becoming requested.

This is very much a result due to the fact that Lena, their data governance lead, has consequently focused on accomplishing value and being of service in changes that have gravity rather than focusing on getting everything right everywhere, or obliging everybody to follow a data governance protocol.

The data governance at Volvo Penta has gone through three phases. Each phase is about three years long.

- The problem-oriented years. Forming a foundation by correcting, simplifying, and consolidating data, and, filling missing gaps.

- The maturing years. Making things easier by improving the operation's performance and introducing improvements.

- Becoming a business enabler. Being a vital ingredient for coping with important business challenges where the gravity is generated. And, avoiding messing things up again when things get tough and stressful.

The Volvo Penta data governance example can almost be regarded as a role model for the four-arena framework for data governance, elaborated in the following chapters. They are *almost* role models, as experiences from several organizations have shaped this framework.

Whitewashing discrepancies

Here follows a neat story of how a diplomatic approach started a movement in a large global engineering company.

The group sales support unit had a problem. On four different occasions, they had tried to implement a common global process for price changes. Not entirely unusual for an international company, they had a rather complicated pricing model, which took both initial sales and aftermarket sales, with spare parts into account. All this was applied on a fairly varied product range. Ultimately, all four implementation attempts failed.

The price data had been changed on local initiatives, which meant that changes in prices were made in an unsynchronized way. Among other things, this messed up the data quality in global contracts, which resulted in extra work on a regular basis. It also led to unwelcome phenomena, such as customers being able to play different parts of the company against each other so that, without their knowledge, they could be competing with themselves. Moreover, the group sales support unit could not monitor price changes, for instance determining whether prices went up or down.

What the four failed implementations had in common was that they all built on a central corporate idea of how everybody should work with price data management locally, rather than on how people actually worked. The reactions had on all four occasions been the same: "we cannot work that way". The reasons for not complying to the process design were recurring:

- how relations with customers were established did not fit the process.

- regulatory requirements in the country of operation prevented such process.

- the business model on their market was different from what the central process required. "We make money in a different way here".

It should be added that this company had grown through corporate acquisitions and had the strategy of retaining well-known brands and the specificity on which they carried out their business. In other words, there was a culture of local self-government in this group.

The idea of getting hold of this was quite simple. Instead of setting the outset from a global standard process that nobody recognized, and even less wanted, they decided to look at what the local discrepancies were really about. Fortunately, at the fifth, attempt the whole approach was completely turned around.

How do you work with price data management?

This task went out to a set of different local units. They were asked to describe how the process typically went on, what could trigger it, what decisions were made, by whom and which systems were used. A template and an example were sent so that the answers would be reasonably similar.

After a while, some thirty different variants of the pricing process had come in. None of them were similar. After going through the material, the group sales support unit saw an almost insurmountable challenge of reaching global conformity in these processes.

It was decided to resolve this in a set of workshops. They gathered a representative from each combination of markets, product lines, initial sales and aftermarket sales. The first task was to go over these process variants to understand the discrepancies. After going through four or five variants, a pattern began to emerge. Many of the differences were of a semantic nature. The names of roles and naming in systems were behind the majority of the differences. What then remained in differences were actual circumstances that could be discussed.

When those who had the greatest differences sat and compared their way of working with each other, the debate became much more constructive and started to include searches for common solutions. Maybe it was the dedication to the group's common quest, maybe, it was the nights spent in bars, but the group started to get to know each other and to trust each other.

It had been quite easy to disregard processes designed at a group function as useless. It was however a completely different thing to defend why one chose to do as one does before an equally wise and experienced colleague.

Gradually, an insight was revealed that discrepancy whitewashing had been a strategy against change. One simply did not have an interest in letting group functions settle in their own affairs for fear of interference from central management in detail local matters. When that honest confession was made, finding what was common became easier.

The ambition was to set up one of the most creative meetings:

Common, but not identical.

And that was all the group sales support unit ever asked for, right from start. When a common process was designed, everything went fast. After six months, the group met again to review how the joint process had been received and what it had led to. It had been used as a pilot in three cases, which led to noticeable improvements in how the collaboration worked and in the data quality.

Almost all of the changes had taken place locally, driven by the participants in the meetings. The central sales support function played a small and coordinated role. The workshop participants formed a network and they continued to keep in contact to learn from each other.

This is a pure diplomacy story. At the outset there was suspicion and, also a little fear.

> *When having unity of purpose, the facts revealed, seeing the "enemy" in the eyes, and, admitting own shortcomings, there was trust.*

And, that was the foundation for change they needed. The diplomacy had changed things faster and with better success than several invasive implementation attempts.

Note that those involved felt that they were working on improving a process, while they in practice were improving how they work with the data. A part of the data diplomacy and non-invasive approaches is to work with people where they are and on their terms.

A traditional data governance approach would most likely have been providing them with standardized data governance roles and expect data quality enhancement from that. That would have been very similar to the previous four failed change attempts.

Almost right data

The following story is not a success story. On the contrary, it is rather a sad moral-learning story but at the same time also includes an example of using an opportunity.

A local logistics company had over 2,000 vehicles at its disposal and undertook all kinds of transport assignments, mainly for short distances. The company has been around for as long as there have been trucks and has been building a rapport with its customers for a long time. The company was owned by the haulers using a membership system.

There were, therefore, quite long and well-established traditions that could not be easily altered. Those who had been there the longest simply knew the best. About everything. When the CEO let his business development manager digitalize the order handling of the trucks, the haulers slammed on the brakes. Paper and telephone were not only safer, but more fun, they claimed. The 2,000 truck computers that were installed were only used as GPS navigators, and not for driving orders. "If I had wanted to use a computer, I would have worked in an office", one of the larger truck fleet owners stated.

Among the permanent customers was a dairy plant that produced cheese. One day, one of the trucks got a driving order to pick up a blue container and drive it to the city dump. The driver noted the container's location and designation on a writing pad, executed the transportation, reported it and the order was billed.

There was just a small problem. The driver took the wrong blue container and did not drive the garbage to the dump. Instead, a well-packed container filled with first-rate cheese was wasted. The driver had carried out the driving order almost correctly. The driver returned to the plant and took the correct container this time. The customer did not have to pay for the extra run, though.

It turned out that the driver had noted the container designation incorrectly. When the designation did not match, he figured it was enough that it was blue, as there just seemed to be a minor data error, again. If the new transport system had been used in this case, the customer would have pointed out exact coordinates to the container location and supplied that data directly to the truck computer, together with the accurate container designation.

The incident quickly spread throughout the organization. There were accusations that some types of drivers were sloppier than others, with the cheese misfortune as a brilliant example, so this was simply expected to happen. As a counter-argument, a group of drivers began gossiping about past errors that everyone else had committed. This led to the insight that inaccuracies occurred almost daily. And, that they were not reported. When looking closer to frequent mistakes it turned out that the cause was often carelessness with data. The data errors were minor, but the consequences could sometimes be immense.

The CEO and the Development Manager used this opportunity. No manual driving orders would hereafter exist. No order data would hereafter be communicated over the phone and paper. Everything would be digital from now on. The order process was enriched with control activities where customers guaranteed the accuracy of the data in each order before its execution. This data was transferred electronically into the trucks' computers.

After a few months they could summarize the outcome. The company turned out to have 15% trucking overcapacity. This capacity was identified when they stopped making mistakes and it finally led to increased profit.

The diplomacy aspect of this story is that the CEO and the Development Manager chose to wait for an opportunity for the change rather than forcing something on the organization that they could not see the benefits of. When the prevailing circumstances became open knowledge, rather than being hidden, a consensus in the problem description came about, combined with a common desire for improvement. As the drivers started to speak truthfully about how often mistakes happened, the communication turned out to be more straightforward. The logistics company was ready for a change. Yet, they lost a dairy customer.

How the truth in the data turned a company

The following story is about how a couple of data architects stopped an investment that could have been disastrous for the company. While the situation took place decades ago, the implications of the story can still teach us something about diplomatic behavior around data.

This happened in a heavy bulk industry company that had been around more than a century. The marketing department had started a program to make the company move more toward its clients and to the market, instead of just keeping focus on its manufacturing and its products. This was well received by the senior management and the group board. This program grew however from being a marketing idea to including sales methods. The salespeople thought that this idea would affect the production planning office which, in turn, thought it would affect the material planning, manufacturing, and logistics which all came onboard with the program.

Of course, there was a titanic system in mind, which was the solution to all the problems all these departments had ever had. They just had to implement it. Everywhere. I was working there as a consultant with a few colleagues, doing our data design thing. We were never supposed to interfere with this giant program, especially not after asking questions like:

"How do you know that this system will fix the problems you are facing?" Or, maybe, we questioned things a little sharper, like

"How can you be so sure?" which wasn't very popular, nor diplomatic. Especially as questions like those were perceived as questioning the expected benefits. This was an important movement that all the managers were engaged in fulfilling. We needed to lay low or be branded as heretics.

We were however concerned. Under the radar, of course, we made sure we acquired more knowledge about what was about to happen in order to get more facts. We quickly got a lead to work on. We managed to persuade our closest customer contact person, who was a manager in the periphery of the big program. He let us participate in one of the meetings with the system's vendor, concealed as data integration specialists.

In that meeting, we asked detailed questions that very few understood the point of, such as:

- "What does the individual product identifier look like, say, for a bulk batch?", and

- "When a batch is divided into individual products, what would those individual product identifiers look like?"

We got away with it as everybody thought of us being geeky and tenacious data specialists. We noticed unwillingness from the vendor to answer these questions, and the managers from the program somewhat supported the vendor, against us and our tedious questions. But we got our answers. After that, we checked the vendor's reference list and contacted a few of them to verify a few things.

What we found was almost a sensation. Something that nobody had thought of. Or, if somebody had thought about it, it was silenced. A kind of "data-gate".

What we found was that the product data structure, the system that they were about to go fully into, was ideal for an assembly production, such as in automotive, furniture, and consumer electronics industries. It supported vast numbers of items that could be assembled in various ways. But our client had only bulk factories. They were working with batches with quality specifications for each batch. Their list of items had just 150 records.

This was bad. The first problem was how to let this bomb detonate. After informing a few of them, who were still our friends, we got our chance at a program director's meeting. We opened by saying the following:

> "Your manufacturing works quite similar to baking buns at home. From a few raw material batches, you make dough. You divide this dough into smaller doughs, which in turn are divided into buns."

We presented a scenario using their own product data, using the generic structure in Figure 1-1.

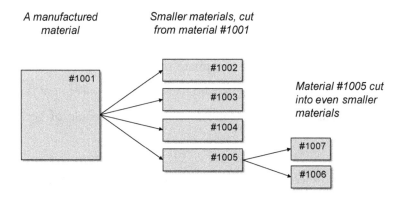

Figure 1-1: A generic view from the company's product data structure.

We continued, showing the next slide (Figure 1-2):

"The system you are about to acquire is constructed for a bicycle principle; you buy parts, which you assemble into components, which will be put together to build a bicycle. This system is constructed up-side down compared to your manufacturing. The system's underlaying data structure simply does not match."

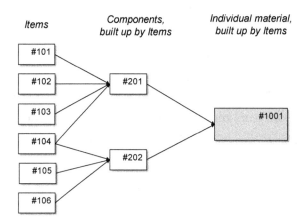

Figure 1-2: A product structure the system supported.

The immediate reaction was that this could not be true, which is a classical reaction of those who do not like what they hear. For if this were true, it could decapitate the entire program. There were just too many managers who had sold their souls to get the program launched to have it swept away by a couple of geek consultants.

We simply referred to the answers we got from the vendor at that previous meeting, and what we had dug up in our research. The vendor was immediately informed so that they had a chance to defend themselves against these accusations. It was suggested that they include all the technical expertise needed to prove that this was wrong.

But the vendor confirmed our findings. They never hid anything. "Nobody had asked us about this earlier", they said.

So, the bomb detonated. The program was cancelled. The program director left the company along with a few more. Many of those who had been heavily engaged in the program went on sick leave or took vacation to take care of their wounds.

Surprisingly, our assignment was not cancelled. We stayed there for many more years and included more consultants. After a year, their standards for managing data and selecting systems had improved, and an enterprise data manager had been installed. A few years later, this new behavior had matured even further and other manufacturing companies paid visits to this company to study data management practices.

What are the diplomacy ingredients in this story? There are a few notable ones:

- **Un-neglecting**. We saw something that caught our interest. We reacted and decided to do something, instead of taking part in a "benign neglect" which would have let an even bigger disaster for this company. My colleague and I were convinced that nobody other than us had discovered these findings; they may have suspected them, but they neglected them.

- **Integrity**. We knew we were right and stood up for it, regardless of whether it meant pressure on us. We were willing to take the consequences.

- **Fact-based**. We never expressed our opinions. We kept everything neutral by letting the facts do the talking. And we knew that we were questioning people's opinions, not their facts.

Without facts, warnings are just opinions. Therefore, always underpin a message with concrete facts. Furthermore, always be crystal clear about what the facts are and what your opinions are.

How Matt unknowingly established data governance

Some data is naturally well managed as there are support functions dedicated to working with it. Employee data is such an example. There is a HR department that manages the human resources, and consequently also the data about this resource. And the need for reusing employee data in various ways within the organization is usually vast. Almost everything that happens in the daily operations is tagged with personnel data to capture "who does what".

Matt is an experienced HR officer. He is employed at the group HR department in a global industry and has a job description that does not keep him entirely occupied, experienced as he is. Soon after starting that job, he realized that the usage of employee data was not very organized. The decision to get data out of the employee master database was purely an integration decision taken by the IT department, meaning, you could get any data you wanted, if the IT department had time to fix it for you. Apart from the security risks, it caused lots of inefficient work as every integration included repetitions of tons of questions such as what the data means, the data update frequencies, and code definitions.

Matt put all the frequent answers into a document. He produced a business-oriented data model and translated it into text so that anyone unfamiliar with data models could get the gist. He made a glossary of all the major attributes and made a definition list of the codes and categories that were used. He had some help in making a second chapter in the document that mapped all this to the database tables and fields (as there were no APIs with standard messages published at this time). Finally, he produced a template so that the HR manager could sign a contract with a data consumer that stated the terms and guidelines for HR data usage.

When this had been going on for a few years, I took on an assignment as a consultant to organize the data governance work. I heard about Matt and met him to have a look at what he had done.

"This is exactly how we would like the data management to work." I said. "How did this happen?"

"I just filled the gap", Matt replied.

Matt was appointed Employee Data Manager in the corporate data governance organization, which was merely acknowledging the work that he was already doing. In the position of Employee Data Manager, he also became a core stakeholder in all major employee data design, including availability and security matter.

Data governance was Matt's job, unknowingly.

Letting it sink in

A multinational food producer decided to give their consumers full traceability to the origin of their food, throughout the entire value chain, from the fields to the fork. Sofie Fischer and Michael Åsman were data architecture leads with this company. They realized that it is not possible to achieve the desirable food traceability without harmonizing the business data. Convincing the managers to invest in data was however something entirely else. But they found a way to succeed with that:

> "Having a business manager doing the talking, rather than an IT representative, has taken the matter of data architecture and data accountability to a much higher level in the organization."

They continue with the importance of endurance and timing:

> "The senior management has gradually realized that integrated processes throughout the group are made possible by the harmonization of data. We were fortunate to create awareness by using tactical timing and giving them time to let it sink in."

One of the diplomatic angles of this was their endurance and timing when communicating what they thought was needed. Another angle is that they found a way to express the value of improved business data design from the viewpoint of the stakeholders. Also, Sofie and Michael let others, who are more credible in business matters, do the talking.

Johan Lindholm, a data governance lead at a utility company, has gained lots of experience from getting quite a few managers to take responsibility for the data their department creates:

> "Being pragmatic and adaptable is the key. I keep the goal in mind and follow the path in a zig-zag pattern, if needed. For instance, if I can't get the proper data stewards or managers acknowledged, I do something else, such as starting an interest group and inviting them as individuals, where I can reach them."

Johan continues with the value of occasional failures:

> "One of the first manager I approached was very positive about formalizing the business data accountabilities and responsibilities and helped me with the establishment. After a while she quit her job and the person who replaced her was somewhat skeptical, regarding data governance as something very abstract. She intended to reduce the scope and the ambition. But it turned out that she also quit her job after a short while. Her successor, the third manager on the same position, was very positive. She thought the messages I brought to her were tangible and helped her in understanding what was expected from her, and why. One conclusion I drew from this journey was that the skepticism forced and encouraged me to become more concrete about what data governance is all about."

CHAPTER 2

Running data governance in four arenas

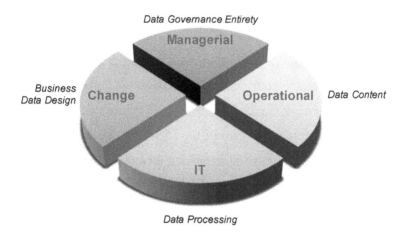

Figure 2-1: **Four arenas for data diplomats. Also, four arenas in a data governance framework.**

So, let us set the stage for data governance that runs on diplomacy. The stage is structured in four arenas:

1. **The Data Governance Entirety arena** is about how to perform data governance and architecture by setting the organizational prerequisites, roles and responsibilities, principles, strategies and plans. And, most important, to

get things moving in a consistent way. It involves the CIO, the data governance lead, data strategists, lead data architect and possibly executive managers from various departments.

2. In **the Business Data Design arena**, the business data is designed. It includes working toward a coherent business vocabulary and a consistent data structure throughout the organization. It also includes working to improve the business data design so that the organization can have the data it really needs. This involves the business representatives who take part in improving the data design assisted by business data architects. This is where the business' metadata is formed, reviewed, decided and forwarded to be implemented in various IT solutions.

3. **The Data Content arena**, where people or computers capture, use, amend, process and send the data. This could include any kind of co-worker, as everybody uses data in the daily business operations. From a data governance perspective this arena includes data workers that directly, or indirectly, take actions for data quality matters. Many requirements toward the data architecture and IT solutions are tracked in this arena.

4. The IT arena, that is, **the arena for data processing solutions**. This where the IT capabilities are made and

maintained. Many detailed decisions about data processing, storage and flow are settled here. Also, many inspirational innovations and insights can be elicited in this arena. Data architects in this arena work typically with designing solutions on a detailed level that are to be implemented into IT systems.

Each of the four arenas consists of different competence areas and perspectives. Different kinds of work are carried out in each arena as well.

> *Ideally, the work done in the arenas is well-integrated, preformed in parallel, and the competences and perspectives are mixed fruitfully whenever any data matter is resolved.*

Any role can share or gain knowledge in any arena as important data matters occur in many aspects, perspectives and detail levels. One individual can perform activities in several arenas, but one individual person should not take full responsibility for more than two at a time as that person might create a bottleneck.

The arenas are illustrated as pies to emphasize that improving the company's data is not an end-to-end process. Such processes suggest that there is a start and a finish, and, have defined points for handing over results. The concept of having data governance in arenas translates into ongoing knowledge sharing.

Constantly sharing knowledge and perspectives is a way to come to the best decisions about how to move organizational data requirements forward.

Regarding the four-arena image as a wheel, this wheel can rotate in any direction. There are however, different kinds of diplomacy jobs in the arenas since there are different goals and different kinds of roles in them.

Other data governance frameworks usually cover three of these four arenas. The missing piece in relation to this depiction of data governance, is the Business Data Design arena. The reason for this fourth arena is that the design of the business' data is not an IT task. It is part of designing a business and thus it is a work for the business representatives. However, implementing this is an IT task. We should regard this arena as the data perspective in business innovation and business improvements, and not as a detail in IT work. From a diplomacy perspective, this is crucial.

The three lower arenas in the figure (data architecture, IT and data content), occur even if there is no formal data governance established. Data structures are nevertheless designed and computerized, while data content is nevertheless somewhat managed.

The description of the data governance arenas continues below, by going over what kind of work is carried out in each arena. In Chapter 3, the roles and responsibilities in each arena is described. But first, let us start with what the work is about and the purposes of the work in each arena.

Data diplomacy does not require a data governance organization. But it helps to have such an organization as it clarifies who to spend time with.

Sometimes, data governance is illustrated as a pyramid. But the pyramid shape can influence us to believe that this concerns the organizational structure when it is generally about competence and cooperation.

Meeting expectations for managing data

Everybody in an organization needs to meet expectations on how to manage data, as, again, everybody is a data worker, at least to some extent. The expectations include security, accuracy, and availability and other typical data governance objectives. The expectations vary with what kind of data it is, and also the context. The expectations are derived from mainly two kinds of sources: regulatory requirements and business requirements. Simplifying things, we can separate it into what the organization must do, and what it wants to do.

- *Regulatory requirements* are what you must comply with, such as laws, doctrines, and industry standards.

Examples: Sarbanes-Oxley Act, GDPR, environmental legislations, and various reporting to authorities.

- *Business expectations* are what you need to fulfill or relate to, such as the market competition, employee attraction, innovativeness, agility, operational performance, contractual terms with partners and customers, and owner's expectations.

These expectations are drivers for data governance. Any goals that are set for data governance are derived from these expectations.

Data governance does however not have goals of its own, such as "100% data quality". Instead, data governance goals are always coherent or derived from the expectations related to how the organization manages its data.

An expectation may be "a customer's claim on a product is to be resolved within one hour" which leaves no room for mistakes or unnecessary actions. The expectations on the data can then, for instance, include that the person who or the function that obtains the claim needs to capture all and only accurate data when a claim process is initiated.

To meet the organization's expectations on data, data governance must include data architecture, which sometimes is, unfortunately, separated from data governance.

Working with data governance includes keeping track of both the metadata and the data.

The "data" is of course the business data, such as "23567" and "978-1-935504-63-4". Metadata is "data that describes data" which in this case tells us that the first piece of data is a picking order number and the other is an ISBN number for a very good book. Data is means and results from daily business whereas metadata is a result from data design, traditionally carried out by data architects.

How data is designed heavily affects the ability to work efficiently with data; if data is designed poorly and implemented accordingly in the systems, the systems will obstruct daily work.

Metadata governance targets the data design including its definitions, structure, labeling, movements and some of the business rules. Data design is typically *built* into various IT solutions, into management systems, and tacit in people's way of processing data.

To ensure proper data design, data architecting occurs in two data governance arenas; both in the Business Data Design arena, as a business design task, and in the Data Processing arena, as a solution data architecture task.

Governance of metadata and governance data require different kinds of skills, strategy, staffing and imply different kinds of outcomes. Hence, they need to form separate arenas. Metadata governance aims to meet expectations in

- proper data design, such as how data is defined, labeled and connected, and,

- how metadata is implemented in IT solutions,

whereas data (content) governance aims to meet expectations on business data correctness, security and availability. Below outlines a section describing each of the data governance arenas. The description includes each arena's outcomes and how to work in each arena. Later, in the next chapter, this description is completed with the most important roles in each arena. There is also a separate section in Chapter 4 covering initiating data governance in a diplomatic way.

Working with the entirety

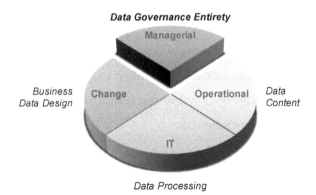

Working with the entirety of data governance means managing the data governance work as such, covering all four arenas. The data governance work needs to be planned, coordinated, staffed, monitored, and improved, like any other kind of operation. A vital foundation of the Data Governance Entirety arena is to define the data governance mission, practices, results, outcomes and the impact it is intended to have on the organization.

Working with the data governance entirety also ensures that data improvement work is carried out in all arenas in a way that suits various parts of the enterprise, their environment and the prevailing culture.

For example, people in the Data Governance Entirety arena cannot "instruct" everybody else on how to do things. That would be very invasive and coercive. Instead, the entirety work is about defining core principles on which data governance is based and helping people in other roles work using these principles.

This arena is deliberately referred as "entirety" of a certain reason. An organization is not autonomous but is a part of a network of actors. These actors interact by sharing data. For example, what happens far ahead in a value chain, both good and bad, may depend on what we do, or do not do. To understand the impact of what an organization does in the context in which it operates, access to data created and used by others is required.

The scope of the data for an enterprise is wider than the organization.

Staffing

Another vital part of this arena is to find people who can take on responsibility of data governance work. Finding these individuals is a challenge in itself. Convincing their managers to let their employees spend time on data matters could be an even harder challenge.

Find is the keyword, rather than *appoint*. In many cases, organizations have made ungoverned improvements because individuals have recognized the need to act more responsibly toward data. Some act this way because it is part of their job description; others do so simply because it is the best thing to do for the organization, their co-workers, the clients or customers, or other stakeholders.

Finding such individuals can give the organized business data improvement effort a flying start since these people understand the work involved and are committed to it. Recognizing them and acknowledging their contributions also provides a positive example to other people who want to do the right thing but may have perceived obstacles to changing their behaviors. This is referred as the Non-Invasive Data Governance[5] concept.

Proactivity

An important task in this managerial arena is to set the agenda for data improvement work on an overall level. This means looking for "gravity" in the organization by keeping track of what important changes and challenges the organization is facing and how they will affect the organization, especially with respect to business data. Such important changes can include product or services development, mergers and acquisitions. They can also be changes driven by technology or regulations.

Being aware of bold up and coming changes enable an organization to be proactive about data governance work. Organizations usually take on larger changes by starting projects. In order to be proactive, roadmaps for data improvements and data governance roll-out plans should be integrated or included in business projects portfolios and IT portfolio roadmaps. Such proactive planning work is vital to ensure attention to the data aspect when things are changing.

---

[5] *Non-Invasive Data Governance: The Path of Least Resistance and Greatest Success*, by Robert S. Seiner. Technics Publications 2014.

Decision-making

Data improvement work always includes many decisions. There are data design decisions, data content decisions, security decisions, and many more.

An important part of the data governance entirety work is to settle the data decision-making. Data matters are a part of everybody's work so decision-making needs to occur within many existing forums and decision bodies. But a few new data governance decision bodies may also need to be formed, especially within the design arena.

Notice that within the Data Governance Entirety arena there are no decisions made regarding data – it is not a goal of data governance to centralizing the data decisions to this arena. As stated earlier, data governance should not be a separate thing. Instead, it is about keeping track of what decisions to make, in what contexts these are made and which decision maker or decision body makes them. And, it is about making sure that certain decisions are made, and not postponed or avoided.

Keeping the data governance lean and fruitful means that decisions about data need to be made close to where those decisions have the most important effects, which is usually also where the best knowledge is. As some of the testimonies in the introduction show, decisions regarding data require tactics and endurance.

The diplomatic way to set up data decision-making is to engage the decision-makers in steps and approach them once there are data matters that need decisions.

Then it will make sense to the organization and be easier for it to take an interest in data decision-making. An invasive and not very diplomatic data governance approach would be an organizational-wide big bang introduction of data governance with a detailed matrix for making any and all data governance decisions. Such an approach would be based on too many assumptions about what to decide and how data decisions really are made. It would simply not work. First there must be something to decide upon. Start there.

Growing

The Data Governance Entirety arena is also about making the data governance work grow in the organization. Data governance work is not static. It changes with the challenges that the organization is going through. It changes as new problem areas arise. It changes as people leave the company and new individuals come onboard. Formal data governance roles can even be reduced, or partly withdrawn, when things are completely adopted or no longer relevant.

Data improvement work needs to advance, mature and widen into new areas. Doing so, it constantly and repeatedly needs to be justified and motivated. The Data Governance Entirety arena consequently relies very much on communicating.

Data governance is knowledge-work. It produces knowledge, it takes knowledge to do it, and the daily data governance activities are very much about gaining, using and spreading knowledge.

Knowledge-work is enriching. It is however also done manually as it is hard, perhaps even impossible, to automate. It is also fragile; knowledge is tacit and personal. Consequently, working with the data governance entirety is fun, slow and fragile.

Data governance management system

Because governance work is largely about communicating knowledge, there is a need for a lean management system as a tool for those who are engaged in data governance activities. It can for instance describe the way of working, and have a set of templates, presentations and reusable material. It can also contain data design results or a direction where to find such resources. Using the diplomatic approach, the data governance management system is not the first thing to do. Rather, this is something you form as you go along. It will be useful when data governance is well established and matured.

Enterprise data model

A part of the entirety work is to be aware of what kind of data there is. An enterprise data model is a way of doing that. An enterprise data model depicts the data entirety at a very high level. It provides a tool for coordination and planning, rather than a basis for something to be built on. Thus, it does not need to be 100% accurate from the beginning. If it needs to be reorganized, just adapt it. Just don't attempt to work out something perfect from start. There are not necessarily many people who completely depend on an enterprise data model in the start-up phase of data governance.

Quite an important aspect is that the enterprise data model reasonably follows the normalization principles, meaning that one type of data only occurs once in the model. That will simplify the data design planning and avoid the risk of overlaps and redundant work.

Ideally, the enterprise data model has the following purposes:

- **Overview of data design responsibilities**. This is about allocating accountability of the business design outcomes. The enterprise data model is an excellent map for showing where the organization has applied data governance, and where it has not.

- **Reference for relating the systems to business data.** The areas within the enterprise data model are suitable to oversee what kind of data the systems are managing. This is useful when talking system landscape roadmaps with other enterprise architects.

- **Coordination of specialized individuals involved.** Both business-oriented and IT-solution oriented data designers tend to specialize in areas that can be mapped to the enterprise data model.

- **Reference for business data design models.** The enterprise data model serves as a content framework for data design outcomes, such as various diagrams, and descriptions.

- **Coordination of planned initiatives.** By linking planned or proposed to areas in the enterprise data model, it is possible to plan for which data and which data models should be reused. It also gives a good picture of which modeling needs to be done, which in turn can guide which individual specialists need to attend through the intersection of project portfolio management and enterprise data architecture planning.

With such a wide range of applications, it is obvious that the enterprise data model should not be too detailed, nor technical. It needs to be graspable, e.g. somewhere between 20 to 40 data areas, and be expressed in a language that fits into the organization's nomenclature.

There does not have to be a single, perfect enterprise data model in an organization but it is helpful to have at least one high-level depiction of enterprise data. There may be other models that are made for other purposes than data governance and thus can be cut in different ways. For example, people within business intelligence may have a similar model that slices the enterprise data slightly different. The database creators may have a different domain division and an enterprise-wide comprehensive model for their purposes and to organize their models.

By being diplomatic in the data governance entirety, you can and should acknowledge that there are these other maps for other purposes. You should be interested in them and establish relationships for collaboration, even though you have responsibility for a different perspective. But there should ideally be only one overall model for each purpose.

Working with data design – change

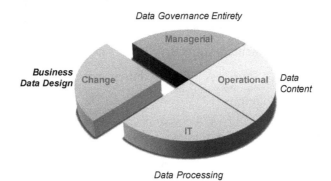

Working in the Business Data Design arena of data governance is about having business representatives taking over the business data design responsibility from the IT professionals. Or, more appropriate, taking back the responsibility as it was probably not delegated to IT in the first place.

The business data design comprises of two aspects of data:

1. Data at rest, meaning the name, definition and structure of the business data, and

2. Data in motion, meaning the data flow and how the data is processed (such as corrected, aggregated, calculated and transferred).

When designing data, you need to start with the first aspect.

The business data design should be a product of those who design the business; those who design how the organization needs to work to fulfill its expectations. Designing the business data must however be facilitated by a business data architect who has the skills needed to ensure that the result is useful, for both business and IT professionals. The result is not something that can be implemented directly; it is rather a result for communicating business data requirements as a base for designing IT solutions.

This is a controversial idea for many. Probably because data storage design and integration design are regarded as activities within systems design. According to the IT doctrine, business representatives, or users, are not expected to be concerned about such things. Since my ideas about data design challenge the accepted doctrine, I'll take some time to explain the detail.

> *Stepping aside from data design yourself, as a data architect, and instead helping business representatives design their data, is an act of diplomacy.*

Data modelers or, even worse, databases designers have traditionally carried out business data design. The latter will of course continue to do so, because the process involves a degree of technical work. But the starting point of what the business data should look like must include the direct perspective of business people. One of the reasons is that there is no quality assurance of the business data structure in having IT professionals ask questions to business representatives, turn their back to them and then producing a detailed system design on their own, solely based on what the IT persons were able to perceive. Such procedure entails basing a design on secondhand facts with opinions and assumptions added.

A great deal of the dissatisfaction with IT systems has to do with the fact that the business data does not really fit into the systems design; important data may be omitted, the system's data structure is not coherent with the reality and may be put in indecorous places, data is labeled confusingly, or, the data design may be outdated.

Insufficient attention has been paid to understanding and getting consensus on how business data looks, how it behaves and what the purpose is of having this data. It even happens that data storage structures come out as a consequence of the system design, as if it were the systems that raise the requirements on data processing, instead of the people who create and use data on a daily basis. Business representatives should not get stuck with systems based on poor data design. Instead, they should take an active part in data design so that data meets business requirements and appropriate system design decisions can be made based on those business requirements and knowledge of the data.

Business data design is about improving the data we have, and, it is about designing the data we do not yet have. Therefore, this is an activity of designing the business.

The business data design is preferably carried out in the earlier phases of change initiatives, for example, as part of scoping and business requirement work. So, instead of asking questions about requirements and then going back to the IT department and drawing data models, the actual modeling work should be done in workshops with the business representatives as active parties.

Succeeding in this, depends on having a number of pieces in place:

- The participants must learn enough about modeling techniques to understand the model they are involved in designing.

- The modeling graphics must be very simple and comprehensible.

- The design outcome must be understandable even by those who did not participate in the design process, that is, understanding in what way the design result will affect the business.

- The model must reflect how the business representatives perceive the meaning of the data, rather than how the data appears in systems.

- The modeling workshop conductor must concentrate on being a facilitator of the data design process, not a data designer.

- The modeling activity needs to stop before it gets too detailed. Generally, business representatives are satisfied when they understand what the data means to them, how it is related to other data and how it is labeled.

Facilitating business data design with representatives from separate knowledge areas, and consequently separate perspectives, is indeed an act of diplomacy in itself. Such a design process unites various interests, perspectives and roles around a business data design the entire organization will benefit from. There is a section in Chapter 4 dealing with conducting such a business data modeling workshop.

A successful business data design

Let's start by clarifying what can be considered as a successful design of business data. Purely pragmatic, the result is a substantially normalized data model that reflects the business data structure and vocabulary from a business operational perspective. As it is the question of design, this result shows how things should look, rather than reflecting it as it is.

A successful business data design leads to a result that the business representatives see as theirs.

The model in Figure 2-2 is a simple example of a business data model that resulted from a workshop. It contains major entities (the boxes), how these entities are structured in terms of relationships (the lines between boxes), a few clarifying examples and maybe a few attributes that have turned up in the modeling process.

The crow's foot symbol in the relationship line end represents a rule that describes the cardinality (one-to-one, one-to-many, etc.) between the concepts in the boxes. Note that when a one-to-many relationship line has a name, it reads from the many-side, called the crow's foot side, of the relationship line.

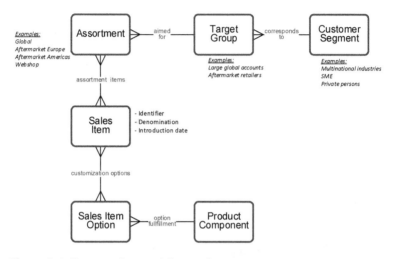

Figure 2-2: Business data model example.

For instance, a Target Group corresponds to one Customer Segment, since there is no crow's foot in the right line end. A Customer Segment may however correspond to more than one Target Group. (Don't worry, I did not get this the first time, either.)

Simply determine if there should be a crow's foot in a line end, or not. In business data modeling it is enough to determine whether two entities have a one-to-one, one-to-many, or many-to-many relationship.

Going further than this is to design systems for data storage and systems behaviors. Let's save that for later.

There is surely a meticulous data modeler that sees limitations and unevenness in the model in Figure 2-2 and thinks "Shouldn't there be a many-to-many between Target Group and Customer Segment?", or, "Why don't you generalize Target Group and Assortment making the concept last longer?" Thinking that way in this early stage might blow away the business' engagement as it then will, again, shift the focus to data storage design, rather than keeping it on business design. A workshop modeling result must not be a perfect data architecture. It needs to have ample business design. The important thing is to decide what data means and how the data is connected.

1. The focus should primarily be on the entities' definitions, that is, what kind of data they represent. Express a few typical examples of the data to clarify the definition.

2. Secondly, such a model should reflect how the entities are structurally related to each other, meaning what consists of what and what exists in the context of what in terms of "one-or-many".

3. Finally, there should be a working and acceptable business name for each entity. Strive to attain a name that will work in the entire organization, not just in one department. This avoids unnecessary misunderstandings caused by synonyms and homonyms.

This is quite enough for the business representatives to produce and agree upon. Going further would be too detailed. Consequently, a business data design activity should, at least initially, leave out the following:

Omit business rules and special exceptions, an exhaustive list of attributes, detailed cardinalities, and data flows in business data modeling. That can be clarified later. Figuring out all that detail would be a waste of valuable workshop time.

This is where diplomacy comes in: the architect who helps the business by drawing a model of their data must reduce her/his own standards for a successful and completed data modeling result.

As a data modeling facilitator, you need to distinguish designing data for business purposes from designing data from system purposes. Designing how a system manages data is something completely different from understanding and expressing how business data fits together.

Introducing business data modeling as a separate activity in a project requires preparation as it may encounter resistance. Some people may question why it needs to be done at all, especially since such a model is not part of the project's final delivery. So, it needs to be proven that making a business data model early in a development work saves time and that, correctly used, it contributes to better project outcomes. This is indeed true.

Designing business data as suggested above is an investment in saving IT projects´ resources. It increases the stability of the requirements, as names and definitions of data are resolved early in the process. It clarifies the scope for the coming systems and the need for integration and provides a reference point for all subsequent project work.

I conduct at least one business data modeling workshop each week (at least half day long) and have done so since the late 1990's. Some weeks there may be even three to four workshops. These workshops have basically been with just business representatives and we model their data together. I have at least 20 colleagues who have the same experience. So, those who claim that this cannot be done are simply wrong. It is easier than playing the violin (believe me, I have tried that too). And those who suggest that these kinds of models are useless can call me, and my colleagues, or our clients and ask if anyone wants their money back. I am happy to supply contact information.

Someone might ask, "Is this not just 'conceptual data modeling?'" Well, what it is called is not really that important; it is what the business data model reflects and the process of making it that is important. The reason for not using the words "conceptual data model" here is because that those words are already taken. And there are many conceptual data models out there that are not the result of a data design process produced by engaged business representatives. Conceptual models are not useful for data governance, as they are usually not normalized enough. There are conceptual models having "Sales statistics" and "emission reports" without resolving what kind of data such reports contain.

When IT specialists dive into a data design that business representatives have achieved, they need to embrace the efforts and be curious about the business requirements. This is a change for those data architects who have the tendency to review, criticize and even correct other people's models. The diplomacy approach does not only apply to those data architects who conduct business data design workshops; it must include the entire community of data modelers and data architects within the organization.

If a business data model lacks in anything – ask. If the model is not sufficiently comprehensible – ask. If it is not clear how the model should be used – simply ask. But do not reject a commitment and time spent simply because a data model does not meet a data architect's perception of quality. Data architects simply do not have a monopoly on data architecture, nor data model quality assessment.

Embrace the progress of having business representatives in the data design front seat, instead of searching for modeling errors in their results.

A business data model is not ready for implementation. There will always be things left to model. There is still plenty of modeling work to do before a system can be implemented. And, as mentioned, the business data modeling process needs to stop in time to avoid the risk of having the model overworked and turned into systems design. Obviously, a solution architect will need to do the systems design, as this involves applying technical knowledge that business people are not expected to have.

Data architects are important and are frequently requested and consequently easily become bottlenecks. Having business representatives taking data design responsibilities can ease the burden of solution data architect's research work, given that the process of data architecture is somewhat amended. It implies a business data architect with skills in working with different people than data architects normally work with today.

Using a business data model

A business data model can be used in several ways to support the other data governance arenas.

Uses of the business data model in the Data Content arena:

- The business data model can be used as a starting point for addressing formal accountabilities and responsibilities for data capture and availability.

- The data that an entity represents, referred to as an entity instance, is captured (or will be) somewhere by someone or something. Before the data design goes too far in the implementation, it is best to check how data will be captured in practice, by whom and in which context. New business data design often lead to changes in the business' processes.

- If we have designed and established a vocabulary and definitions, they should also be implemented in the organization, where needed. It also includes wordings in management systems, documents and spreadsheets and, by extension, terminology when people communicate.

- The data will be enriched during its lifetime. Data will be added, and relationships to other entities will be established. This will be done by people or by computers. Either way, these steps and events need to be known. The business data model can be a starting point for understanding enrichments and the model will evolve as these are documented within it.

Uses of the business data model in the IT processing arena:

- The business data model expresses business requirements. Having the definitions and the vocabulary in the model enhances communications concerning requirements. (See "Fact-based business requirements" in the Toolbox chapter.)

- The business data model is useful as an input for further requirement work, such as data security, data constraints, data flow and functional requirements.

- Validation of requirements – ensuring the right requirements are set. For instance, by producing test data examples from various business scenarios that might arise.

- Verification of fulfillment of requirements at a commercial off the shelf (COTS) or a built system.

Uses of the business data model in the Data Governance Entirety arena:

- Putting the business data model into a repository enables reuse of knowledge in future and parallel projects. This may require some model management, for instance making new material fit into existing material. Ideally, existing models should be taken into account during the data design process and not afterwards.

- In order to achieve stability and significance in the design result, the structures, definitions and vocabulary may benefit from going through a review and approval process. This would pave the way for the common direction of essential data, such as master data. This, of course, requires an established data governance process, which we will come to next.

Getting the proper representation

Data crosses all kinds of boundaries. The same data, or the same kind of data, can cross organizational boundaries, and geographical boundaries, and thus also system boundaries. There are also boundaries constituted by people's professions; there are specialized vocabularies connected with job types. A field service engineer, an accountant, a purchaser, or a manufacturing optimizer have separate specialized terminologies, which are not always consistent.

The work on designing data cannot therefore be done in an isolated part of an organization. It must always be linked to a context and existing data in order to be meaningful in more places than it appears. This insight is a vital part of the job as an enterprise data architect. As stated earlier, data architecture is, after all, not only a design role, but also a coordinating role, and sometimes also a facilitating role. A single enterprise data architect cannot her/himself take responsibility for the accuracy of all kinds of data design in the organization.

The solution is to ensure that a broad set of perspectives influences the design of business data. That means getting input from a range of people when designing data. The sample model in Figure 2-3, which is similar to the one a few pages ago, depicts Sales Items. That is, it answers the question, "What do we have for sale?" This is data that naturally needs relationships to other data. It is for instance related to product development data to understand what lies under the magic that we sell. Also, we need to relate what we sell to finance reporting. Furthermore, it is also possibly related to ordering, order execution, logistics and invoicing. Sales Item is typically core and widely used business data.

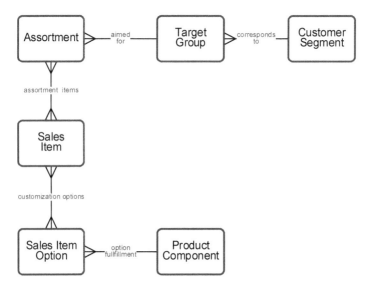

Figure 2-3: Sales Item business data model.

Thus, changing the definition, the attributes or the data range on Sales Item cannot be made in isolation. Ok, it sounds like we need to invite a lot of people to such data design activity.

When planning for a session that requires wide representation, there is a small trick: do a draft model to figure out what kind of related data must exist when a Sales Item, an Option and an Assortment is created. For example, there must be Product Components available, because otherwise there is nothing to make Options from. Okay, therefore, invite people who work where the Product Component originates from. If there is a hard and direct dependence downstream, such as sales order management, then it may be a reason to invite people even from there. This can be enough to carry out initial workshops and a first data design. After that, the result can be matched with representatives of other perspectives in shorter meetings.

Importantly, those who work where the data naturally appears must influence the design right from start.

The business data definition is applied where the data is originated.

This basic principle is very useful, understandable and unquestionable. It harmonizes well with the entire data diplomacy philosophy to get first-hand knowledge as a strategy for "doing things right from the beginning". Always ask those who know, not just those who have opinions.

Getting a proper business data design is all about having the right people influencing the design.

Picture a situation where a sales rep becomes acquainted with a person at a marketing event. They talk about their purposes of being at the fair and discuss common interests. At some point, they exchange contact information and the sales rep makes a note of the meeting and a quick assessment of how this new relationship may evolve. If she or he thinks there are reasons to follow up the meeting for a possible future sale, the sales rep has unknowingly applied a couple of entity definitions. In that moment data for the entity "Sales Opportunity" and "Potential Customer Contact" is originated, and thus the definitions are applied at that moment. Just imagine having someone else other than the sales reps, such as an accountant, defining what "Sales Opportunity" is and relating data to it. Or a data architect.

Designing different kinds of data

All data cannot share the same data strategy, do not need the same attention, and do not require the same data governance ambitions. Consequently, depending on the kind of data, the investment in efforts and technology will differ. For instance, the following varied examples would require different kinds of activities:

- digitalize a frequent reoccurring manual process
- improve common master data
- improve business monitoring
- collect data from equipment remotely
- produce a report for management
- taking a note from a meeting.

These examples will all address different kinds of data, and, that will affect those who are active within data governance and their type of engagement.

As a diplomatic data design facilitator, you will benefit from understanding what kinds of data there are and how data governance should affect them. Having that understanding, you can explain what needs to be done and why to others. Giving people knowledge by teaching them new things is a way to gain trust and to have influence. The two following sections give guidance on how to recognize what kinds of data there are, and how these kinds can affect how you work with data governance.

This section deals with two ways of talking about different kinds of data:

- Data that has different kinds of lifecycles, such as long or short in a small or big volume.

- Data that is shared, and, data that should look alike, meaning, shared definitions.

Data lifetime

There are several ways to categorize data. Very often data is categorized by the data consumption, that is, categorized by who is using it, or, who is originating it. This is usually aligned with which system the data resides in, and, what department is managing the data. But this does not tell us very much about how the data behaves, that is, the lifetime of subject the data is reflecting.

Based on the lifetime, there are four distinguishable basic data[6] types:

1. Category data
2. Resource data
3. Business event data
4. Detail operational transaction data.

This classification is vital to the planning of data governance and data design work since different types of data require different approaches. First, let's define the data types by their lifetime.

---

[6] *Enterprise Architecture Made Simple*, Edvinsson & Aderinne, Technics Publications, 2013.

Data types	Examples	Volume	Growth
Category data	• Customer Segments • Product Group • Mode of Delivery	Few values	Seldom
Resource	• Sales Item • Employee • Customer Vehicle	Many	Follows the size of the organization and business volume
Business Event	• Sales Order • Delivery event • Customer's claim • Payment	Very many	Follows (is) the business volume
Detail Operational Event	• A phone call interruption • The clutch pressed down in a vehicle • Geographical movement • Post on a social media	Vast	Growth increases with the business volume

Table 2-1: Types of data discriminated on lifestyle characteristics

Let's explain these four types of data from Table 2-1: [7]

- **Category data.** Data used to classify and assign types to things. For example, customers classified by market categories or business sectors. Product categorization is another example.

- **Resource data.** Basic profiles of resources need conduct operational processes such as Sales Item, Customer, Supplier, Facility, Organization, and Account.

---

[7] *DAMA The Data Management Body of Knowledge*, Technics Publications 2017.

- **Business event data**. Data created while operational business processes are in progress. This type of data glues daily activities together into business processes. Examples include Customer Orders, Supplier Invoices, Cash Withdrawal, and Business Meetings.

- **Detail operational data**. These types of data are produced through social media systems, other Internet interactions (clickstream, etc.), and by sensors in machines, which can be parts of vessels and vehicles, industrial components, or personal devices.

The difference between these data types is the lifetime of the subject the data is representing. It is consequently, not how long the data is kept; a piece of data can be interesting and valid for a very long time for historical reasons. Rather, it is the lifetime of what the data reflects that is interesting. A business segment or a line of business (categories) may last for a century, a vehicle and an employment can last for decades (resource), a sales order may be processed in hours (event), and, a weather sensor can supply a temperature reading in a second.

Note that the definition of these lifetimes varies with the type of industry, or even with companies. For instance, the definition of resource data is not likely to be the same for a government, a bank and an online sales company.

The **category data** values seldom change. Within business intelligence these are often referred to as slowly changing dimensions. Categories always have something that is categorized, such as business segments to categorize customers and lots of other elements we wish to place in a segment. This data do not have a process creating them, in the way that most other kinds of data does; they are developed or fall into disuse as a business and its data grows. We, the humans, have a natural habit to simplify things through categorizing when things become complicated and overwhelming. Important category data can simply just occur.

Have a look at the business data model in Figure 2-4 below. The "Customer Segment" entity is a typical categorizing entity having maybe just four to five values. They may occur on external websites, in tons of spreadsheet files, in business warehouses, and in finance and ERP systems, among others.

There are a few important aspects when designing or improving category data:

- Data governance concerns the name and definition of each category value. The definition of a category includes the value range of the data being categorized.

- Reflect whether the category values are of company common interest – if so, they probably occur in lots of places already and may unfortunately take years to unify and cleanse.

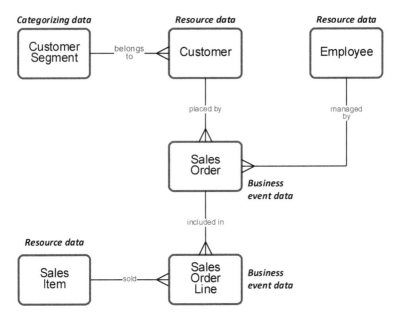

Figure 2-4: Sales Order business data model.

The **resource data** is often referred as "master data". Calling it "resource data" is simply because this kind of data reflects various resources. Resource data is traditionally the target for master data management and master data governance. Master data has however a wider definition than reflecting resources: "master data is the data we chose to manage in master data systems" which could be any kind of data.

There are a couple of important aspects when designing or improving resource data:

- Be sure to understand where the data is created originally. There is usually a process to establish this kind of data. Be aware that the human awareness about a resource is usually much earlier than it is put into systems. It tends often to take a quite long time in the process between something important has happened before the data is recorded. For instance, an employment can be offered and accepted at one point of time, and may be documented in a system days after, which is a quality loss.

- Business interests are often about the data definition, data structure, categorization and naming conventions. Just think of the perpetual discussions about the "customer" definition.

- Also, determine whether the data is of global/common or local interest (more about this in the next section).

The **business event data** is often referred to as "transactional data" among IT professionals. But "event data" is more encompassing. This kind of data reflects various business events and is not limited to transactions. Transactions refers to systems' communications and is a much wider concept as any kinds of data may be transferred. As mentioned, this type of data is a business process carrier. A Sales Order for example, is typical business event data as it carries the execution of order management and keeps the sales order activities together forming a process. Business event data is typically the target for digitalization.

There are a few important aspects when designing or improving business event data:

- It always has at least one relationship to resource data. It connects the business process to data about the who, what and where of the process.

- Business event data always has important data about "when" things happen. A business event entity always has an important date attribute. Ideally there is data about "how" and "why", too.

- Striving for standardized business data definitions does not necessarily imply standardized processes. The data structure needs to be designed so that it is neutral to how the process is performed. That way, process changes do not have to mean dramatic data changes.

The **detail operational data** does not have a generic name within IT, but this type of data usually adds up to what is called "big data" due to its massive growth in data volumes. This data is often produced by various devices, or, by large amounts of people who leave traces in social media, web visits, pods or blogs. There is an important aspect when designing or improving detail operational data. Business representatives should be able to influence how data in technical devices is architected. The data design in sensors, engines, portable devices are usually architected by the engineers constructing the technology. Without a business perspective, important contextual data can easily be missed which reduces the potential value of the data.

Figure 2-5 is an overview of the four data types.

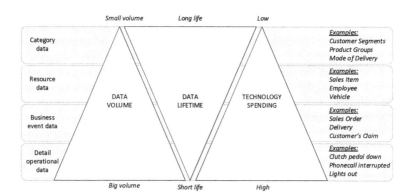

Figure 2-5: Overview of the four data types.

For each data type, the triangles reflect high and low data volumes, the long and short lifetime the data is reflecting, and the spending in technology. Most spending is put into digitalizing the business event data and detail operational data; we automate frequent processes and we control, monitor and log by introducing Internet of things (IoT) technology rapidly.

Applying modern technology to collecting valuable data we never had is indeed fascinating. But we cannot forget the category data and resource data, since ultimately, the business event and detailed operational data represents things that happen to resources of different categories.

Since we spend a lot on technology for fast and big data, manual work remains for managing small and slow data. Data governance is therefore very relevant in digitalization for enabling big data to become knowledge.

Common data and shared data definitions

"Sharing data" usually means two things: using the same data definition, and, using the same data content. These are two completely different things. In this section, we work out this and present a model for dealing, and perhaps negotiating with it. The model can be used for several purposes, such as:

- To determine what data should be shared or commonly defined.

- Settling differences in interest between central and local parties.

- Settling difference between data architects and business representatives.

- Consequently, setting the right limits for data sharing.

- A starting point for setting strategies for different kinds of data.

- Explaining and motivating such strategies.

Data sharing means that you are using exactly the same data. Data definition sharing means that you are using the same definition but not necessarily sharing the data.

Let us start with sharing data definitions. Using the same data definition means common terminology, data structure and thus the possibility of using a common system. For instance, two subsidiaries can share the same CRM system as they have a similar conception of "customer", but do not need to share the data about activities regarding their customers.

Sharing definitions implies having a common vocabulary.

Architecting data includes defining the business meaning of the data. A part of the definition consideration is to determine whether the definition should be wide and generic, or, be specific. The designation assigned to the data, also known as the 'label' or 'data entity name', is usually the way to determine the definition.

In Table 2-2, there are a few examples regarding various parties a manufacturing company is interacting with.

A generic definition will include more data than the specific as it will include a wider range of data. Also, a very generic data definition will include more people and types of professions.

Accordingly, a more specific definition will give meaning to fewer persons which is not very useful.

Specific definition	Typical data modeling generalization	Very generic definition
Main component supplier Software supplier Office supplier	Supplier	Party
Large accounts Global accounts Dealer Medium-sized customer	Customer	
Authority Bank Journalist	Interested Party	

Table 2-2: Generalization levels on kinds of parties

Nobody says, "Today I am going to have a meeting with a Party". I will probably meet with a customer, a dealer, a supplier or a bank.

"Party", the most generic example, requires subcategories. The data may need to be organized at several levels. Moreover, there are consequences with having too many generic definitions, and, also having too many specific ones:

- The more generic a data definition becomes, the fewer people will be satisfied with the definition and the labeling of the data.

- The more specific a data definition becomes, the less reusable it is and the more difficult it is to compare across data sets.

The advantage of generalizing is to cover more data in an IT-solution and thereby reduce costs. Data architects are therefore willing to generalize and handle specific definitions as categories and subcategories. But the reality is often more complex than that. To generalize means to simplify. Not only do IT systems need to be cheap, they also need to be able to provide support in complex contexts. It is therefore often a struggle between the architects' willingness to simplify and the challenges of the business with complexity.

Let us move on to sharing data. Some data is common, other data is not. Data concerning sales items, the organization's structure, customer segments and the profit centers are typically shared data. These kinds of shared data are also usually centrally created and managed in larger companies.

The opposite, the unshared data, is data that could very well be accessible but not of immediate interest to perform the daily operations. For instance, a meeting with a client implies data about who is meeting who and where, and, includes a calendar booking. Who uses this data except for the people attending the meeting?

Combining specific or generic data definitions, with high or low data share, we get four fields of data management situations. There is no good or bad here, just different challenges. This model is intended to be conferred when setting targets and strategies for how to cope with various data management challenges.

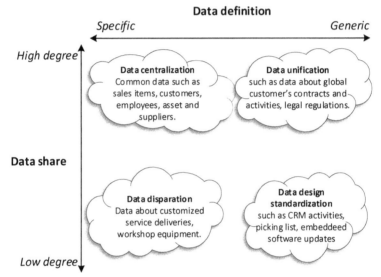

Figure 2-6: Four fields of challenges.

It is inspired by Jeanne W. Ross's operating model[8] covering process integration and process standardization. Like in Ross' model, this model does not have a "magic quadrant", indicating that one quadrant is better than the others. It is simply four directions that are described to simplify quite complex conditions.

---

[8] *Forget Strategy: Focus IT on Your Operating Model*, by Jeanne W. Ross, MIT.

Data centralization is about striving for high degree of data sharing, meaning, that as many kinds of data as possible should be accessible, usable and meaningful for as many as possible. We strive for common definitions and common data. The resource data of common interests (explained in the previous section) typically occurs here.

Data disparation is the natural behavior for ungoverned data[9]. Without guidelines, we do whatever solves our problems, as we are not aware of what happens simultaneously with other clients or at other plants. Data is locally defined, captured and stored. For example, a local unit uses centralized data for sales items and financial terms but captures disparate data for everything that is unique in that unit's environment. What happens in local businesses can however be of central interest but because the data is not defined generically and is not shared, it is very hard to compare it to and relate it to other data. Disparation is not only caused by geographical distances, it is commonly caused by organizational units or professions.

Data design standardization is about using standardized definitions without sharing data. In this situation, the definition of the data is standardized regardless of what process it is used or captured in, or wherever the work is performed. The

---

[9] *Data Resource Quality: Turning Bad Habits into Good Practices*, Michael H. Brackett, Addison-Wesley Professional, 2000.

standardization of how the data looks enables central monitoring and reuse of supporting IT-system, even if two local offices or two parallel processes do not share their data. This is very useful when having replicated local units, such as retailers and local service units.

Data unification is about everybody using the same terminology and data definitions and sharing the data. Data may be captured centrally or locally. Processes are enabled to be fully integrated. This usually works well for some of the financial data, like the general ledger. It can also include global customer contracts, legal data and common regulations. The ambition to put everything in this corner is often the enterprise data architect's dream. It is also very rare to have it like that, unless you are very small organization.

A classical direction for data strategy is to keep a combination of data centralization and data standardization. Typically, this means having selected category and resource data centralized and mastered, and business event data locally captured and for local eyes only. This model can be used for forming data strategies, such as deciding what kind of data should be managed according to what quadrant. Such discussion could include sharing data and definitions in central, global and local management, data crossing organizational borders or professions, or, any combinations of these.

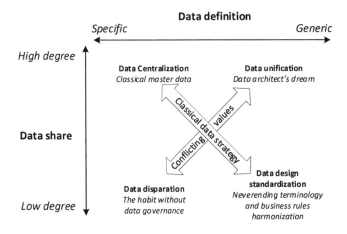

Figure 2-7: Data negotiation model with typical standpoints.

Working with this model can bridge differences between business and IT, and between local and central management.

Working with data content – operational

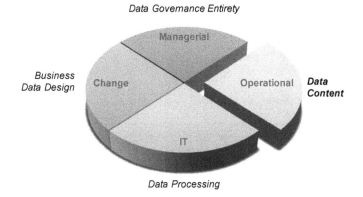

The Data Content arena concerns the data as such, and not the metadata or data models. In this arena it is about managing the business data as a part of the daily work, or rather, managing data is usually the daily work.

Data content management is sometimes confused with data quality management. Data quality management is an extensive topic with lots of theoretical models and approaches, all aiming for the same goal: reaching high data quality according to data quality measurement specifications.

In this diplomatic approach to data management, the "data quality" topic is rationalized and simplified:

Your job includes data. Simply do your work as it should be done and the data you create will be of high quality. Improve it, if needed.

There are those who suggest that data quality rates are the ultimate measurement of the success of data governance. That cannot be true. The only thing that such measurement indicates is the success of data quality efforts.

Data quality is not a measure of its own right. It is a performance indicator that needs context. Data quality rate can however be used to estimate operational efficiency.

Data supplied to other parties and data stored and made available for use are however expected to be correct, complete and consistent. Not only for regulatory reasons but also for safety, contractual and efficiency reasons. That means that there should be quality checks in data flows or workflows. But it does not imply that all data needs to always be 100% correct and complete everywhere.

The diplomatic approach brings a few messages in the everyday data content management context:

- Nobody is called a data manager. Very few claims to work with data content. A construction engineer and a salesman do not see themselves as data content managers. Yet, almost everyone is a data manager working with data content.

- Regard data capture, data improvement and data availability as a natural part of work being done. Thus, integrate the data quality perspectives whenever doing work improvements instead of having separate data quality activities.

- Reduce risks for data quality shortcomings and improve the workflow efficiency by enhancing the "I" in "IT-requirements".

- Cooperate with entity managers and data architects when defining data requirements for IT systems. They have much to contribute.

- Organize the data improvement work by applying a few useful principles instead of focusing on separate data management roles.

Data content real-life cases

Here are a few real-life cases describing how to do data quality work pragmatically:

- Ove oversees product documentation at the product development department in a global industry. His team is managing product data that is provided for sales, logistics and manufacturing product data. "We know we have some data quality shortcomings in our product construction structure database. Some items are outdated, and some bill of materials are inconsistent. But as long as nobody suffers from this, we won't spend time correcting it."

- A key account manager in the same company as Ove keeps track of and logs his sales activities in a CRM system where he also constantly updates the predicted value of the sales opportunities. He is aware that the accuracy of his forecast figures is questionable. And, there are some performed sales activities that are not recorded in the CRM log. So, that kind of data, which he is the obvious originator for, is neither always correct nor complete. However, each piece of data in the customer contracts is 100% accurate, simply because the expectations on that data quality is much higher.

- Eva works at an IT services desk in a bank's back-office function. One of her tasks is to manage user accounts. They have many older systems that do not work with modern user catalog services for single sign-in so some user administration needs to be managed manually. Since it is a bank, user authorization is indeed important, both for enabling employees to carry out services and to prevent misconduct by the bank's employees. As things are supposed to work, every time there is a change in an employee's job function, the user authorization needs to be immediately amended. Especially when someone leaves the company, the access to the systems must be revoked directly. The problem is that Eva is not always informed when people quit or when their responsibilities are reduced. Many attempts were made to fix this, mostly by trying to straighten up the procedures when an employee leaves, such as introducing checklists of what to do. Automating this was not feasible as the criteria for reducing accesses could not be defined in a deterministic way. The pragmatic way to solve it was having Eva take charge of quality checks periodically. Every six months, each department manager checked the job function of their staff against a list of employees' accesses to various systems. Eva provided the list and updated the access based on the result from the checks. So, the pragmatic way was to accept a portion of low data quality for six months. This was easier than trying to induce people to report every change in the workforce as they occurred.

Data content management principles

As shown in the various examples above, it is not possible to form a generic process for keeping data accurate. How this process is applied in each case depends on what kind of data it involves and what degree of accuracy is expected, desired or required. This is where data governance can easily become a bureaucracy.

To avoid that, principles can be used instead of attempting to form heavy data quality procedures. These principles can, in turn, be used to form procedures for a management system, job introduction or form IT-requirements to support systems. There are, of course, cases where rigid data controls and checks are required. But getting things right and efficient can be accomplished using principles.

Principles are based on values. Business rules are based on principles. Stating principles can thus be a way to simplify things.

Data content management principles include:

- Trusting people
- Always the right data from me
- Capture data close at the spot-of-origination
- Opportunity is power.

Trusting people is a part of the diplomatic approach. In data content management you assume that employees want to and strive to do their work well. Doing things well includes doings things well for more than yourself. It is also important to do things well for people who are depending on what you are doing.

"Always the right data from me" is a pragmatic principle based on the assumption that nobody wishes to create issues for others. Everyone takes the responsibility of always delivering correct and consistent data to downstream activities. A giant furniture company resounded this principle throughout its organization and consequently gained a notably improved performance.

The principle of "capture data close at the spot-of-origination" definitely applies to data content management. Everything else than data at the source is secondhand knowledge and thereby a quality risk. Close to the natural source of data means:

- where the data is naturally created first, as a result, or a log, of an activity in a process. Examples include a customer asking for a quotation, and the quote provided.

- where it is discovered for the first time, such as measured. Examples include a measured volume of fuel in a storage, or the weight of a newly developed product.

- where it is determined, as in a result from a decision. Examples include the acceptance of a vendor's offer, the setting of a maximum load weight, and the determination of the sale price of an item.

- where it is processed, not just aggregated (manually or automatically), but with judgments added to it. Examples include forecasted sales figures and a production plan.

This means that, with all the best intention, the person entering data into a system should preferably be a part of the occasion, or the event, when the knowledge arises and consequently can be captured as data. Putting it on a piece of paper and handing that paper to another person is begging for quality risks.

Following the spot-of-origination principle for capturing data derives from another principle: assigning accountability for data.

The accountable for data content is a manager of those co-workers who are responsible for capturing data at its point of origin.

Another principle is "opportunity is power". Anyone who discovers something bad should be able to fix it immediately. If it cannot be done, then at least the responsible person is notified. Everyone contributes to making everything better and does not neglect something important. The habit of neglecting issues and errors is fatal to the overall performance.

Again, having a diplomatic data governance approach is not narrowed to avoiding errors. The starting point for securing data is therefore not a rigorous control system where someone checks what others have done. Rather, it is about providing employees and data suppliers with high quality standards, with the support they need and trusting people. Quality systems are usually designed to find errors. The diplomatic approach proposes that it should be easy to do things right in the first place.

Data quality is not equivalent to the absence of errors. Achieving high data quality is meeting expectations. Therefore, achieving expected data quality should be about how we do the right thing. Not about avoiding doing wrong.

Working with data processing – IT

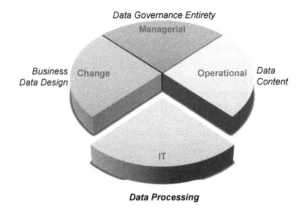

Data Processing

A great deal of demands on IT solutions crop up in the Business Data Design arena and the Data Content arena. These become requirements that are expected to become reality in the Data Processing arena. This arena is where blueprints, such as data models, become constructions. This is where the detailed requirements are defined and implemented into systems, which will have an impact on daily work for the rest of the organization.

If the other arenas are working properly, the chances of doing things correctly right from the start within IT increase tremendously.

If the other arenas manage to come up with consistent and coherent results that can bring value to the organization, it should be just a walk in the park for IT to implement these. Now, why is that so?

"How hard can it be?"

As mentioned earlier, a great deal of the dissatisfaction with IT systems has to do with business data not fitting well into the systems design. One explanation is that insufficient attention has been paid to understanding what business data looks like and how it behaves. A major goal of the diplomacy approach is to fill that gap.

It is, however, quite understandable why IT professionals do not take time enough to analyze what business data looks like. Just consider what characterizes "good" system development. By "good" we usually include accurate functions, technical robustness and high tolerance of user misuse, which of course are all important. But it makes the programming profession devoted to write codes that is able to cope with any possible exceptions. This is where the largest workload lies.

Thus, some system requirements are about what a system should do, but even more about what it should not do. The business representatives usually have their greatest interest in what a system should do and how that would improve things, while system builders spend most of their time on what a system should not do.

Furthermore, the goal for IT professionals is to supply suitable IT solutions. The motivation for business people taking part in data design and data content management is to have better support for the business data in order to meet expectations in the organization.

The first step to diplomacy is to understand, and then acknowledge, that we have separate motivations.

Typically, neither side sympathizes with, or tries to understand, the other perspective. Business representatives often regard IT work as slow; "I know what I need. It is not that complicated. How hard can it be?"

IT professionals, on their hand, often refer to people that work in the operations as "users" who act inconsistently and do not always know what is best for them. "We constantly get conflicting requirements from different departments. And then the requirements change. Just figure out what you want. How hard can it be?" This is of course an exaggerated and prejudiced description. But still not unusual.

When there are separate motivations, there will be differences. Where there are differences, there will be conflicts. Hence, diplomacy is needed.

There is consequently a need for data diplomats to act as intermediates between business and IT.

Both sides are, however, often united in the pressure of reducing costs. Unfortunately, that fuels further problems. When there are cost reductions in the daily operations, there are usually reductions in manpower, which calls for more automated work and investments in efficiency. Meanwhile, if there are reductions in IT spending, there are not enough resources to automate and invest in efficiency.

Improvements in operations are however not only achieved through new systems. There is much to be gained by consistently having the right data and thus reducing unnecessary work. The Data Content arena overcomes that.

Getting the most out of IT investments is basically about the same thing; making sure to do the right thing from the start. The Business Data Design arena addresses that.

The Data Processing arena also considers how those who buy, build and integrate IT solutions can cooperate with business data designers and business data content workers.

Benefits for IT processes

The demands on how systems need to be improved become more clear, pragmatic and distinct when you have well-organized data content work. Without this, situations can be cloudy. IT professionals work on detailed levels and need to understand exactly what is wrong with the system if they are to address issues. The conversation may otherwise be very undiplomatic:

"The system contains bad data."

"So what? Just stop putting bad data into it."

A person actively responsible for data content and knowledgeable about business and technical processes can often get insight into the kinds of improvements that will reduce errors. Such a person may express demands in a more diplomatic way:

"We can reduce manual data entry checks in system A if the system would do a consistency control against system B. Also, if the system could make sure that the field NNN is not left empty, we would reduce hundreds of unnecessary phone calls each week."

These are suggestions and not complaints. They center around the data, and, there is a small business case motivating the suggestions. And, these suggestions do not blame anyone for buying or building a bad system. They merely observe how to make the system better.

A diplomatic example

A recent case shows how dissatisfaction with IT gave way to thinking in new directions resulting in a win-win situation. It took place at a utility company whose infrastructure grows by close to 10% annually. The company tried to keep its network documentation up to date. It had a brand-new IT-system for network documentation and a small group of full-time employees to keep the documentation up to date. They were provided with data by the field installers who sent in notes and drawings of what they had built. But the documentaries complained that the system was hard to use, especially given the large volume of information they had to document. There were very many hearty complaints about the system as the stress of having a constantly increasing backlog grew.

An expert who analyzed the situation, saw that the reason for the system being perceived to be sluggish was because the documentation required was actually quite extensive. The solution was however as elegant as simple. Instead of letting the documentaries do all the documentation, they let the installers do it in the field. This simplified the process and enabled data capture at the point of origin. The field people were already at the source of the data, so the quality of the documentation also improved. The system came to fruition as this was how it was built. The documentaries went on to support the field workers with their work. The problem was that they have acquired a new system but had remained with a process optimized for paperwork. In this case, there was dissatisfaction with IT but a process improvement created two winners.

Introducing data diplomacy in the IT arena

In the IT arena it is indeed important for data governance representatives to have a service-minded attitude. Data governance representatives can easily be regarded as authorities and fault-finders instead of guides and knowledgeable resources.

Bridging the business data architecture with IT solutions, data architecture implies that bridging normally goes two ways. That bridge can hence be used in both directions. There is a lot to learn from experienced solution architects. There is a lot to gain from having well-organized data management work as an input to, or a part of, IT work. Following the principle that "data governance is not a separate thing", the IT side also needs to be prepared for such an engagement. Below are some diplomacy features that make life easier to fulfill the data governance intentions.

When everything is working well, this is how it is done.

- We include data perspectives when planning IT. That means that every IT project or IT activity is well aware of what kind of data it is about to take on. This can be made possible by having each project portfolio using the enterprise data model to show what data is targeted, improved and used. Data is a part of a project's scope.

- An IT project hosts Business Data Design arena activities. Business data modeling is done as a part of understanding and clarifying business requirements.

- IT professionals can distinguish between business design data models and IT-solution data models. Both kinds of models are most likely produced in the same project.

- IT professionals embrace business design data models.

- Data migration toward new business data design is a part of IT projects' deliverables.

- Data content responsibilities for new data business design is also a part of IT projects' deliverables.

- The IT solutions are mapped to the business data models verifying the outcomes from the projects.

- Data models are stored to be reused in other projects and in IT maintenance. All changes in reused models are updated. If a model is governed, the changes are also approved.

In addition, many insights from business data management are useful for IT on almost any level, such as:

- overall enterprise architecture matters such as determining what data each system should manage,

- integration considerations including what and how data should be transferred and consistency checks between systems,

- authorization and security, like who should do or see what,

- detail requirements such as automating data checks for reducing data errors.

Many frustrated data modelers have spent a huge amount of time with business representatives to come up with an excellent model. But, since they have not spent time with the IT teams who will implement the model and did not prepare them for how to use the model, the implementors skip it and re-do the whole thing from their perspective.

Given these conditions, a diplomat can face many challenges in the IT arena. For instance, it is common to have a solution architect on an IT project. That person is focused on the project's results. Enterprise architects keep the entirety in mind; the entire organization's data including the data in value chains and end-to-end processes. Sometimes, these two perspectives are on the same track, but sometimes they only meet occasionally at the same spot. So sometimes they are enemies. For the same reasons, a solution data architect can come into conflict with an enterprise data architect on how data design should be implemented.

There are a couple of typical reasons for this. First, it is a symptom of having disparity in requirements from business representatives. If this occurs, they could be fighting someone else's war. The working methods in the business design arena try to impede this.

Another reason is that data architecture concerns often appear too late in the project. When data design is done by architects, and not modeled with the business representatives, at least one of the two architects has got things wrong. Maybe both.

Making agile methods diplomatic

When agile methods came about, retrospective architecture meetings also came about aimed to ensure architectural compliances and to keep control of the ongoing projects. Such meetings are often an inheritance from project gates, which are quite popular project management tools. The project's results are controlled, checked against agreed standards and sometimes questioned in such architect's check-up meetings. Every check that does not pass will result in a change request in order to meet the architect's standards. Those kinds of meetings tend to be reactive, formal and sometimes picky.

The whole purpose of these gates and reviews is to keep the system landscape consistent and coordinated. The only way of achieving that is by closing the knowledge gaps. It does not have to be undertaken in a reactive way.

As an act of diplomacy, these could instead be prospective meetings. This means introducing all the relevant business data models to the projects in the early phases and indicating where to find everything they should be aware of. That means that requirement analysts, project lead architects and the solution data architects can have the correct knowledge from the start by reading and digesting things that have already been settled. Closing the knowledge gaps like that save a large amount of time.

Additionally, there is a possibility of reducing heavy change request processes. Digging into models and enhancing them leads to more insights, which in turn can be reasons to change existing systems.

A change request process concerning an existing system can include many roles commenting, granting or preventing changes. Having all four arenas represented can provide a shortcut; simply include the people who are concerned from the other arenas and discuss the matter as soon as a potential change is encountered. This could resolve the matter easier and quicker. If a change is required, the change request will be much better prepared.

CHAPTER 3

Organizing the four data governance arenas

Typically, the main function of data governance frameworks is to control and check what people are doing. Such an approach takes a rigorous set of procedures, checks, roles and rules. There are multiple problems with this approach: it includes clear signals of mistrust, it will easily become a bureaucracy, and it will move the focus from the data toward the control system. An overdesigned data governance framework contains rigorously detailed roles, placed in a structure on at least three levels and with decision bodies on all levels. It is characteristically filled out exhaustively with precise criteria of who appoints who and when to escalate to each level. Maybe it is the word "governance" in it that makes people motivated to invent a domestic system of justice.

Such a data governance system of justice is only about preparing for failure. Instead of getting ready to face an organized crime, let us increase the chances of doing things better.

In this chapter we will delve into how to organize data governance work, in "just enough" size, and, to strive for improvements. After all, diplomatic data governance is about initiating, guiding and encouraging people toward better behavior regarding data that benefits the entire company and its stakeholders.

Roles overview

Below are the most significant roles in a diplomatic data governance structure. Each role is defined from one arena, but any role can appear, interact and communicate in any other arena.

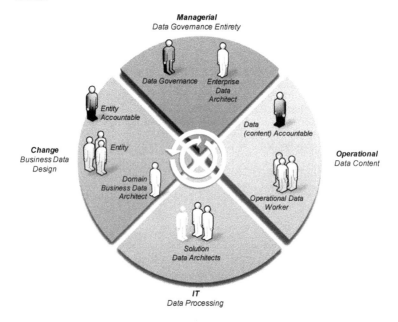

Figure 3-1: Overview of roles in the arenas.

As mentioned, a person can play more than one role, and, occasionally more than one person can share a role. More roles than these can be active, take part and contribute in these arenas in various activities. We will have CIO's, enterprise architects, data base designers, and so on, regardless if we run data governance, or not. They would do their job in quite a similar way anyway, albeit somewhat affected when we introduce data governance. Some of those roles may also hold a data governance role.

Below are descriptions for both accountabilities and responsibilities, so let's start by figuring out the fundamental difference between them.

"Responsibility" means making sure that things are happening and that results are achieved. Responsibilities typically apply close to the sharp end, where things are happening. "Accountability" includes a funding aspect which implies justifying the cost for the activities or what they may imply. As the data diplomacy approach addresses behaviors, the focus here is on responsibilities.

Roles in the managerial arena:
- **Data governance lead** – the executive data governance officer that directs data governance operations and strategy, and coordinates people and activities to meet data governance goals.

- **Enterprise data architect** – the overall data design ward coordinating data governance's and data architecture's results.

Roles in the change arena:

- **Entity manager** – a business representative that is responsible for the data design in a data domain.

- **Entity accountable** – a business manager that enables entity managers to be active.

- **Domain business data architect** – a data designer that facilitates entity managers' work.

Roles in the operational arena:

- **Operational data worker** – a person that has a responsibility of accomplishing correct data as a part of her or his job function.

- **Data content accountable** – a business manager that is accountable for data quality as a part of his or her job function.

Roles in the IT arena:

- **Solution data architect** – a person that designs technical data solutions based on business data design and other requirements.

The following sections deal with these roles and describes what they do, how they act and how they interact.

Organizing the Data Governance Entirety arena

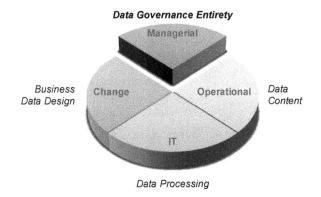

Data Governance Entirety

Data Processing

Organizing the data governance entirety means organizing the roles, procedures, decision-making and other prerequisites in all arenas, included in this pie chart.

Data governance must have a leader. This is an Admiral without an armada. This leader is preferably already within the organization thus aware of the core business, has a network and is aware of the organization's natural behavior. This leader needs to be supported by a knowledgeable consigliere[10], an advisor, who could be a coaching consultant, whereas the data governance lead should preferably be an employee. To be practical, these two roles could be referred to as the data governance lead being the Admiral, and the enterprise data

---

[10] In the Godfather novel, written by Mario Puzo, there were consiglieres giving advice to the leaders. Some were suited for peace time, others for war time.

architect as the advisor. The rest of the people active in this area are already hired as managers and co-workers, data architects and various IT professionals.

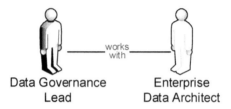

Figure 3-2: The Admiral and the consigliere.

Having just two main roles who act for the entirety is quite lean. If the workload for these becomes too heavy, as it can become in larger global companies, the data governance organization can have multiple instantiations. That would mean having more than one pairs of Admirals and consiglieres, for instance for separate business units which do not share very much data.

Taking into consideration the mission and the task there is, however, no need for more active heads in these roles. They should not do more than necessary, and they should not be loaded with work that is not about the data governance.

The role of data governance lead

The data governance lead is the driver of the data governance initiative. Having this role, you set the level of ambition for the data governance and how it should evolve. The data governance lead is a promoter and encourager of data governance without interfering in detail matters.

The data governance lead paves the way for data governance work. Typically, the data governance lead is heavily involved in finding and including individuals to be engaged in the business data design and in the business data quality.

Once individuals are found and engaged, they need a context to work in. Paving the data governance way is a full-time job. Fortunately, not everything needs to be done at once. The data governance lead is one of few roles that could work full-time with data governance.

Maintaining data quality in everyday work should, as mentioned, be regarded as part of the daily work. Thus, it cannot have any separate control, but should be integrated into the existing management systems. No new managers are needed for this, but rather it is about adding or adjusting how the management is conducted. Thus, a data governance lead needs to ensure that this happens.

The diplomatic approach with governance thus means coaching leaders to improve their data governance. Not bringing in new governance.

Undoubtedly, the best opportunities for improving the data assets are when something is subject to change, when there is gravity. Therefore, it is crucial that data governance has an impact on the change processes. From the earliest phases and throughout the change process, there must be clear elements on how to improve the business data whereas other changes are formed and launched. Data governance has no better arena for significant progress than here. Thus, a data governance lead needs to ensure that this is enabled.

The diplomatic approach thus means helping improvement in respect to data.

Data governance lead funding

To achieve benefits, awareness and, in the long run, a lasting change, a dedicated data governance department is not required. The important thing is: what is done and where it is done.

Successful data governance work can be organized in network form; a network of knowledgeable people who are spread out but who can be linked together in some way for common matters. Data governance can also be formed as a set of guidelines describing the way of working and provided with knowledge support. There needs however to be some kind organizational mechanism to have access to the members in the network when needed. There is however still a need for someone to drive the process as culture does not change by itself.

Some believe that the data governance lead should not belong to the IT department, while others claim that the role is definitely a strategic IT role. But it doesn't really matter where a data governance lead is placed. Home is where the work is[11]. The most important thing is that the manager of the data governance lead values the data governance work and ensures that she/he get the best conditions.

There are those data governance leads who have a budget, own resources and an allocation in the line organization, including a formal mandate and a marked accountability. There are both advantages and disadvantages to having it that way.

The benefit of this approach is that there are resources and power when needed. It is also favorable for the coordination of ongoing activities. Additionally, it is easier to build up competence when keeping the active data governance people together.

But one should pay attention to the risks of referring data management and its resources to a single place in the organization. The other parts of the organization can perceive that they do not have to worry about data architecture and data quality as there is a special department for it. Another risk is that the organizational boundaries can become obstacles when there is a need to make some sort of correction or adjustment; it is

---

[11] *RecrEAtion*, Chris Potts, Technics Publications, 2010.

seldom popular to have one department interfere in the responsibilities of another department. A special data quality department that also has a mandate to enter wherever it is needed can easily be perceived as a regulator, rather than a partner. The biggest risk, however, is that such a department is peripheral and isolated instead of being a natural part of ongoing operations. Such a peripheral group can easily be questioned and become extinct in the next reorganization.

The role of the enterprise data architect

While the data governance lead is the figure that drives, engages and promotes data management activities throughout the organization, the enterprise data architect is the one who organizes what the data management should work with. An enterprise data architect identifies information areas, subject areas, entity areas, data domains, or whatever they are referred as where you live, as a world map of the organization's data assets.

An enterprise data architect is aware of how the organization's data is handled and has a general knowledge about which data is vital. This means knowing what the current situation looks like, including strong and weak points. Like the data governance lead, or perhaps through her or him, the enterprise data architect has knowledge of the coming challenges that the organization will face and what data is required to meet these challenges.

As indicated when introducing the Business Data Design arena, we need a set of business-oriented data architects. It is necessary to organize them in order to meet the business's challenges. One way to divide the data architecture work is to specialize in different data areas, such as Customer Data, Product Data, or Financial Data. Another is to work with different business areas, which can, for example, be different types of offers or customer segments or product lines. A third way is to act as an internal consulting organization and act as a knowledge resource when needed; having data architects with broad and generic skills but however not too specialized.

No matter how this work is divided, an architect or team of architects needs to provide an overall picture. Doing so is normally the responsibility of the enterprise data architect or the enterprise architecture team.

The Diplomatic Enterprise Data Architecture

The enterprise data architect not only needs an enterprise data model. A person in this role also needs to know how to use such a model. An enterprise data model is not, as some people think, "The Model", you know, the overall blueprint that should be implemented throughout the entire enterprise, using force, if needed. Those attempts occurred during the information-engineering era in the 1980's. The reason that was stopped was because such work was endless. And, there was no receiver, customer or user for such an enterprise-wide data model. Except for the person who created it, of course.

---

*The enterprise data architect is **not** the person that architects the entire enterprise's data assets – he or she is the person who makes sure these data assets are architected.*

The person who is acting as the enterprise data architect may occasionally step into a data design role and for instance support a project. But the primary role of the enterprise data architect is to coordinate and coach the data architecting efforts throughout the enterprise. This implies that, ideally, the enterprise data architect has both architecting skills and leadership skills. It is perhaps not the best architect that is the best lead for enterprise data architecture.

The enterprise data model is a great tool for the enterprise data architect. In a start-up phase, it is a good idea to organize the contents of existing data models, according to the enterprise model areas, by splitting them up to fit into the areas. This helps clarify the enterprise data model and enables any previous work to be reused. The data architects who once drew these models will feel honored and be glad to have their previous results reused.

An enterprise data model can be expressed as a data model, which is a diagram depicting the structure of how data is connected. But the easiest way is to have a list of data areas, sometimes referred as subject areas. Using graphics is of course preferable. The small example in Figure 3-3 below is a set of data areas, each formed as a box.

Commercial Organization	End Customer	Supplier	Own Organization	Work Force
Service Offer	Sales	Purchase	Target	IT User
Product Offer	Product Price / Cost	Manufacturing Order	Technical Service	Work Order
Product Design	Individual Product	Stock	Product Usage	Product Concern
Product Assembly	Product Aftermarket Preparation	Logistic Unit	End Customer Contact Event	Location

Figure 3-3: Map of data areas in a manufacturing company.

There is no particular order of the data areas in the diagram but there are a few principles outlining how they are organized in the picture.

- The data areas that reflect master data (slowly changing data that is commonly used) are placed along the edges.

- Product master data are placed on the left, master data about parties are placed at the top and geographical master data at the bottom (with a few examples). Some use colors to reflect this.

- The data areas that reflect the business events (data keeping daily business processes together) are centered in the model.

These principles are merely good practice and each organization should develop its own layout standards. A benefit from using a common layout standard when drawing larger business data models is that it facilitates readability. Especially in a large organization, this kind of consistency can help people more quickly understand different models.

Each data area can contain a data model. As data governance and data design proceed, the granularity level on this model can increase since after a while we will need higher resolution in what we are governing.

The enterprise data architect requirements should set the level of ambition for the work on business data design. This implies that all those who architect data in the organization have a role in supporting the overall enterprise architecture.

Organizing the Data Design arena

Because many organizations do not run business-oriented and business-represented data design in a structured way, it is worth spending some time thinking about how to organize the data design and change arena. This section is centered around the entity manager, a central character in business data design.

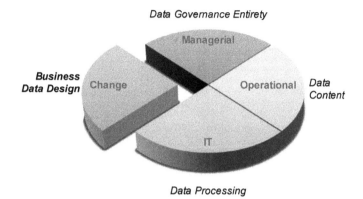

The entity manager – finding the hero

The group of people who participate in data requirement work and in business data design meetings is usually temporary. When the work is done the group evaporates. Their sense of ownership for the result is thus short of duration and fragile. This may not come as a surprise as data modeling is hardly what they have spent 10, 000 hours on doing. They just go back to their "real" work.

The trick is to find and grab a candidate entity manager in this group who may take over a lasting responsibility for the business data design results.

An entity manager is a role within data governance that takes responsibility for the definition, structure and designation of business data. This person is not an IT professional. Rather, this person works in the actual business and probably has done so for a while. A perfect entity manager is

- well-experienced in her/his field,

- has first-hand insight into the challenges that the organization is facing, or is about to face,

- has opinions about how things are done, and ideas how things should be done,

- is broad- and open-minded,

- has been in a "misery zone", meaning, has experiences from data-related things that went seriously bad,

- is trusted by others,

- can cooperate with others.

Such a person may be talkative, but he/she could also be an undiscovered superstar that has not yet had a breakout at the proper arena. But the odds are that this is most likely a heavily occupied person.

Then it remains which entities this person should manage. Again, follow the principle of managing quality where the data is created. A set of entities whose data is created in the same part of the organization where the person works, can form an entity area. This grouping can be influenced by, but should not be completely ruled by, the enterprise data model.

"My passion for data structures and data quality brought me into entity management which turned into a career path."

Joachim Bondeson, Process Manager and Entity Manager at Volvo Penta.

The example in Figure 3-4 below depicts "one entity is managed by one entity manager". That is of course convenient but not always possible. It works quite well for kinds of data that originate at one place in the organization or in a well-standardized process, such as data about products, physical assets, employees, suppliers and ledger accounts. But for data that is captured in many places and in many different ways, such as data about customers, work orders and logistics parameters. it is not as easy to find just one person to manage that single entity. In those cases, entity management can be staffed with a small set of representatives each covering their area.

An entity manager manages mostly metadata (definitions, relationships, etc.). The operational data itself, that is, the data, is usually managed by other people in the organization (refer to the Data Content arena described shortly). One exception is entities that reflects category data, such as "Target Group" in the example model in Figure 3-4. In these cases, the category value set is managed by the entity manager as the value set constitutes the definition of the entity.

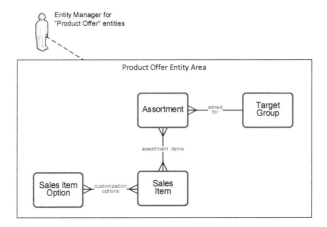

Figure 3-4: A group of entities managed by an entity manager.

Entity accountable

Having an entity manager, it is quite easy to find the entity accountable: just appoint the closest director above the entity manager. Here, the role is deliberately referred to as entity accountable and not Entity Owner, as an employee does not own anything that in fact belongs to the company.

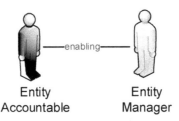

Figure 3-5: An entity manager is acknowledged by her or his boss.

The mistake often made is to first appoint an entity accountable who in turn appoints entity managers, without either of these understanding what it is about. The result is rarely successful.

Entity managers are best found, not appointed. People in this role need to already have a high level of understanding of the data, the processes that create it, and the uses to which it is put. As noted earlier, an entity manager who has been tempered in a 'misery zone', through experiences of things that have gone wrong with data, will be better prepared for this work than one who has not gone through that kind of experience.

The most important task for an entity accountable is to allow entity managers to engage in enterprise-wide data matters and spend working hours on these. Simply find the proper entity manager and appoint her or his boss as an entity accountable.

Later, in a more mature state, the entity accountable may be asked to do some measures and guidance about business data directions. But this is not required in the early phases as it is usually about first getting the basic data to work as it should. So otherwise, don't bother the entity accountable very much.

Designing business data properly takes knowledge, not rank.

Business domain data architects

> "Architects refers to the art and science of building things (especially habitable structures) and to the result of the process of building – the buildings themselves." [12]
>
> *DAMA DMBoK2, Data Architecture Chapter*

According to the DAMA Data Management Body of Knowledge (DMBOK2), architecture refers to both the ideas and to the results. That applies very well on the perception of data architecture. The DMBOK2 states that data architecture encompasses three essential components:

- data architecture results (drawings and specifications),
- data architecture activities (fulfilling intentions) and
- data architecture behavior (mindset, skills and collaboration).

This harmonizes very well with the diplomatic approach of what to expect from a data architect. In order for the business data design to become a reality, it will require all the usual architectures within systems engineering. Typically, it is the architect who, as in art and science, is the author of the design of data processing. The diplomacy aspects appear in the third bullet above, the challenge to stand back in the art process and adopt an interpretive approach to the creation of business data.

---

[12] *DAMA Data Management Body of Knowledge*, 2nd edition, Technics Publications 2017.

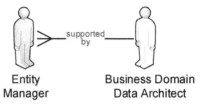

Figure 3-6: An entity manager is supported by a data architect. Read the relationship name from the crow's foot.

The entity manager is supported by a diplomatic data architect who needs to have the ability to interpret the entity manager's perception of how the business data is organized and how it should be developed into understandable business data models. And to do this without influencing the result too much.

Finding suitable business-oriented data architects is just as important as finding the right entity managers. In addition to being capable of changing from designer to the supporter of the method, the architect must also be:

- **Communicative** – this work is mostly about communication.

- **Interested** – being able to listen to what is said, and almost said.

- **Experienced in data modeling** – being able to translate thoughts into graphic structures quickly.

- **A comprehensive thinker** – able to keep the whole organization in mind – that is avoiding data design from becoming too local.

- **Enduring and patient** – it takes time for business representatives to enter business data design mode.

- **Committed to the goals** – by guiding the business representatives into accomplishing a feasible and yet audacious enough data design.

A data architect with these characteristics will naturally influence the work. And that is okay. Facilitation does not solely mean reflecting what is being expressed. It also means influencing a wider and forward-looking perspective. The diplomacy part is in the ability to balance between leading a group to a solution rather than imposing the architect's own solution. In the beginning, the person playing the enterprise data architect role may act as the business data architect and thereby set the standards for others. When the business data design process has matured and more and more areas are modeled, it is a good idea to divide the work between some facilitating data architects. These architects can divide the work into domains within which they develop their specialist knowledge.

How to cooperate in the Business Data Design arena

Five roles have been presented, so far:

- The data governance lead
- The enterprise data architect
- The entity manager
- The entity accountable
- The business domain data architect.

They all have work to do in the Business Data Design arena. How to cooperate can be determined using a set of principles, described below.

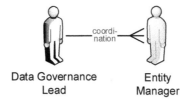

Data Governance
Lead

Entity
Manager

Figure 3-7: How entity managers coordinate.

The initial main task for the data governance lead in the Business Data Design arena is to scout for possible entity managers. This takes a lot time spent on tracking and enquiries. Possible candidates are preferably invited to contribute in business data design in areas that still lack a person with entity responsibility. The selection of people for such work is therefore almost strategic, at least tactically important. The data governance lead will need to use, and indeed also extend, his or her network in the organization. It is time-consuming work, as each new person she/he meets needs to be presented and convinced of the benefits of doing business data design; including business representatives.

Once up and running, the data governance lead needs to ensure the entity manager involvement in various development initiatives. This is one of the main tricks of having engaged and active entity managers: keep them busy and they will remain in your business data improvement movement.

Active entity managers prevent having data architects as bottlenecks.

The data governance lead needs to make sure that the entity managers are not too busy and turn into bottlenecks themselves. The entity manager might also undertake other kinds of roles like a product owner (a project or system role), a project steering committee member, and also digging into the data as such, thus becoming too busy.

A rule of thumb is that an entity manager should not hold roles in more than two arenas.

The key to reach enterprise-wide data consistency and coherence is progress in a coordinated way. This can be done in a non-bureaucratic way.

Check with others before closing a data design process. Correcting later will take more effort. Bad design consumes more efforts than getting things right from start.

But everybody is busy, and in particular the entity managers are busy as they are people who are often in high demand to start with. Any coordination effort needs to be lean and brief. The following way has proved to meet this.

The trick is to keep track of these relationships. Both entity relationships and human relationships.

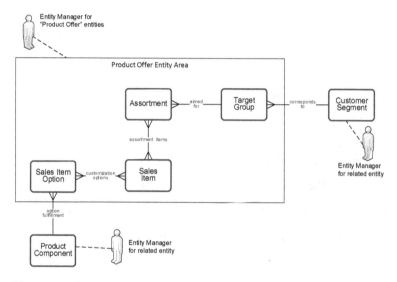

Figure 3-8: How entity managers relate.

No business data is autonomous. No data model can therefore be autonomous. No system data contents can be autonomous. Use the business data model to understand who to coordinate with. Data crosses borders, so do people. Because data entities are related to each other, entity managers must be connected to each other as they manage their data. Thus, each entity relationship to another entity area implies a connection to another entity manager.

As soon as a data design changes or a completely new business data design emerges, these related entity managers should be:

- **informed**, if we want to use their data in a new way. In particular, if we want to process it further,

- **committed**, if their data needs to look different, or, contain something more, or less, to fulfill our new design,

- **activated**, if our new design will mean changes for other entities.

As an example, if the entity manager in charge of "Product Offer" entities intend to introduce Target Groups as a sub-division of the Customer Segments, a logged email informing the entity manager of the Customer Segments would be sufficient, if the formalities require so. But if the Target Groups require a new Customer Segment data value, it will require a committed entity manager to do so, or to reject such a request.

The data architects, if they have split the responsibilities by domains, need to relate in a similar way. As they are a little bit more committed to data models than the entity managers, they may discover the need to initiate and promote cooperation and relationships between the entity managers.

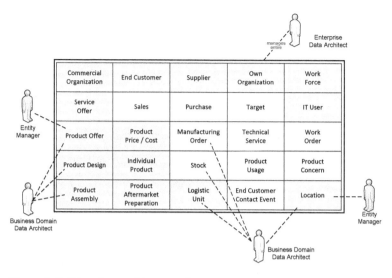

Figure 3-9: How data architects and entity managers cooperate.

So how big is this data network? The ratio between the number of entity managers and the number business domain data architects is on average 10:1, having approximately ten or so entity managers supported by one business domain data architect. And there may be from one to around 20 data architects in a Business Data Design arena where at least one should be the enterprise data architect.

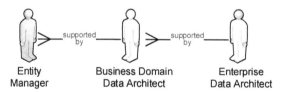

Figure 3-10: How data architects and entity managers cooperate.

Consequently, when fully organized, we are talking possibly hundreds of entity managers in a large organization. That is why entity managers need help from the business domain data architects to determine who to coordinate with and when to connect with their counterparts who have responsibility for other entities.

The business domain data architects need help from the enterprise data architect who is responsible for setting the scope of what the entire network should focus on. The data governance lead needs to keep track of the entirety, such as how the coordination works, how the people who need to be engaged are activated, and how to ensure engagement for emerging data areas.

This might seem a little complicated. Once this is working, it is quite simple. Start with understanding what kind of data is being targeted when a business data design initiative is about to begin. Include responsible and affected entity mangers in the work and select what business domain data architect should facilitate. Go from there according to the principles above.

Making business data design decisions

With a network of hundreds of people, of course, the question arises: "who decides?" However, it is not that complicated. Two things are needed: a decision-making body and a decision preparation process.

Let the decision to adopt a data design be close to the data source. Thus, engage the entity managers in the decision-making. Do all the work in the preparation process so that people understand the context and the best option, and the decision meeting is only formal.

The decision-making body for data design is, in its simplest and most effective form, a collection of entity managers. The implication from this is that the entity accountable is delegating to the entity manager to make the data design decisions. The decision-making group can be built up by a business data domain, that is, a few areas from the Enterprise Data Model.

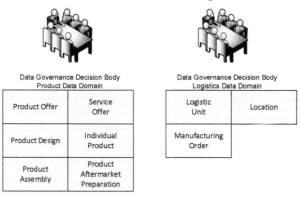

Data Governance Decision Body Product Data Domain			Data Governance Decision Body Logistics Data Domain	
Product Offer	Service Offer		Logistic Unit	Location
Product Design	Individual Product		Manufacturing Order	
Product Assembly	Product Aftermarket Preparation			

Figure 3-11: Two parallel decision-making bodies for business data design. One for Product master data (left with only gray entity areas) and one for Logistics data (right).

Any governance body set up to guide business data design will need a mandate to make these design decisions on behalf of the entire organization. This mandate needs to come from the highest possible level, such as a strategic decision-making body with at least C-level participation. The delegation is typically proposed and prepared by the data governance lead as a part of the "paving the way" work.

The boundaries and interface between the delegated data governance decision bodies can be defined and influenced by the enterprise data architect. The trick is to avoid stove-piping between these decision bodies is to use the entity manager's co-operation principles mentioned in the previous section. The decision body should follow the data, not the organization.

Someone important should be the chair. Possibly, a CIO. Not the data governance lead, at least not initially, as this may be perceived as invasive; the data governance lead would then both be paving the way, and striving for his/her own power. Maybe the chief enterprise architect would do given that he/she is in a position of authority in business matters and is a person of standing.

Note that these decision bodies are not staffed with the entity accountable but with the people are used to be included in data design.

The data governance lead sets the agenda and prepares the meeting and makes sure that the proposals are ready for decisions. Each decision proposal is submitted by an entity manager and is prepared with support from his/her regular supporting domain data architect.

The main idea of making the preparation work brief and lean is to have the proper involvement and participation in the data design process. As mentioned earlier, those who are affected by a change in the data design have either participated in the modeling, or, have had the opportunity to validate the result. Compliance and alignment to existing decided models is settled during the design work. The support data architect does this in the background while modeling.

Apart from the data design, the decision preparation process needs to include the following steps:

1. Clarifying what is being changed, such as an existing data design, or a decided business data model (if it has not yet been implemented).

2. Producing an understandable description of the design proposal.

3. Having the design checked by issuing the proposal to concerned parties, such as related entity managers and data consumers.

4. Resolving technical implications such as what systems, data hubs and integration that will be affected.

5. Checks against parallel ongoing data design and implementation work.

These steps do not have to be carried out in this particular order. They can be rearranged, depending on the change being addressed. First, there needs to be an as-is and a to-be description, which are steps 1 and 2. Producing an understandable design proposal description can be done using a "Data Model Story" (see Chapter 4). Resolving technical implications should not be the responsibility of the entity manager. Rather, an IT-oriented architect will determine where, when and how the business data design proposal will be implemented. The design check with parallel ongoing design work is easiest to do while designing the proposal.

When all this is done, the entity manager can bring the prepared proposal to decision. The decision meeting will then be just a formality. The design has already been worked out, verified and validated in various contexts. As a formality, the chair checks that all steps above have been taken and then asks all delegates individually in the decision-making body if they grant the proposal. If so, it is passed, and the decision can be communicated and put into work.

The chair does not need to engage completely in the decision material. It is enough just to trust the entity managers and that the process is working. Decisions may include:

- A business data design, such as an improved CRM data model, a changed customer discount rule set, a product designation convention, a customer loyalty data structure, or, a unified data model for product construction and product assembly.

- Changes in values in governed Category Data Entities (reference data values), such as the name and definition of a new Customer Segment or the data naming of a new product line.

Category Data values (often reference data), such as customer categories, can sometimes be hard to distinguish whether there is an entity in its own right, or, a value in a category entity. The difference is usually a matter of generalization, or convenience in separating responsibilities among the entity managers. The values can be defined and decided in the Business Data Design arena, or, in the Data Content arena.

Organizing the Data Content arena

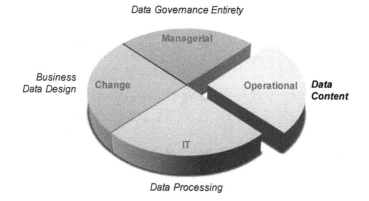

Data Governance Entirety

When organizing the Data Content arena, one cannot rely only on the business data models; capturing, using and processing data in daily operations does not really correspond to normalized data. Rather, data content needs to be understood in terms of workflow, business process and data flow. Data models can however be used to clarify what kind of data is being managed within these flows. As mentioned previously the best way to get high quality data is to get first-hand information.

Capture data once near its spot-of-origination.

That means get as close to reality as possible. This is also valid when defining the data conceptually; go to the spot where the data is naturally created and let the people in that environment determine how the data should be defined. In this way, information for data definitions can also be sourced first-hand. It is preferable to assign responsibility for data quality in the context of where data is captured or created.

Since each organization is unique, the organization of operational data content also becomes unique.

When applying a Non-Invasive Data Governance approach[13], one avoids appointing people into a data governance

---

[13] *Non-Invasive Data Governance: The Path of Least Resistance and Greatest Success*, by Robert S. Seiner. Technics Publications 2014.

organization top-down. Rather, one strives to find those who are already doing important data work, formalize that work, and acknowledge the contribution of those that do such work by assigning them a data management role, if needed. Not only is this non-invasive and non-coercive, but it is also diplomatic.

Avoiding "stewards"

The "data steward" is a frequently used term within data governance. Traditionally, it is a role that cares for data, from various perspectives, toward the expectations on data governance, such as improving data quality. It is, however, omitted here of several reasons.

First, the "steward" part of role name is indicating that it is someone that is wiping someone else's mess, similar to a steward on a Caribbean cruise ship. Even regarding the data stewardship as an administrative role indicates that it is a role dealing with a separate thing from the business operations.

Secondly, it is a role that is designed for data governance and is not a term that neither the business or the IT sides can relate to.

Moreover, what the role implies is not easy to adopt. If you are a line manager for an office dealing with customer's claims, you are probably not recognizing your work as a data steward. The data in your office is just a reflection of the work you are dealing with, not a separate thing. Keeping track of the office's performances and how well it meets the expectations include, or should include, data quality measures combined with other indicators. As stated already in the introduction, everybody is a data worker. Stewarding data may be what we already are doing; simply do your work as it is expected and the data you create will be of high quality and available in time.

Roles do not improve things. Activities do and responsibilities makes activities happen.

If there are problems with the data, it is not only about correcting it, which a traditional data steward would be dedicated to. Rather, it is about preventing it from being incorrect again. Picture two teams that have similar tasks and the same prerequisites, but they perform their tasks differently; one team exceeds expectations and the other one performs low. We may very well be thinking of two teams that are resolving customer's claims. Let us say that the second team is late when delivering data, does not comply to standards formats, and often omits data. Monitoring the data quality, data standards compliance, or data delivery accuracy may be a way to monitor the team's performances, together with other measurements. How would we improve the performance in the second team? Probably by letting them learn from the high-performing team, combined with coaching activities, and investigate if there are any obstacles preventing them from performing.

Examples of organizing customer data and product data

Below are two examples of organizing the accountability and the operational responsibility for data correctness. In both cases, the business data models help to visualize this accountability.

In this first example, a company's market structure corresponded to the organizational structure and thus the operational responsibilities, as shown in the data model in Figure 3-12.

Each market unit has a responsibility to develop its own market. Account managers at the market units, who find, establish and maturate customer relationships, undertake this development. As these account managers are very close to the natural spot of customer data origination, they become responsible for customer data quality. In this real example, this formed the basis for data content responsibilities, as the data structure was already coherent with the organizational structure.

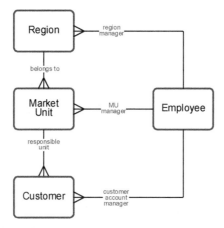

Figure 3-12 Data model describing part of a commercial organization.

As shown in Figure 3-13, the regional manager became accountable for data correctness and completeness while the account managers became responsible for accomplishing it. The middle manager was given a coordinating role.

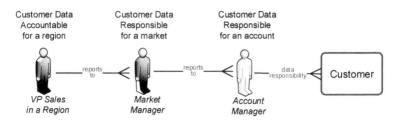

Figure 3-13: Data responsibilities following the organization.

As one of the regions was covering the European Union, this distribution of data responsibilities was driven by GDPR[14] compliance reasons. The managers' data responsibility included not only a customer master data database table, but all data regarding the customers.

The CRM data model for this customer concerned more than just the GDPR scope. As shown in Figure 3-14, almost all sales data related to customers was included in the data responsibility. And, not shown in this figure, much more data related to this was included, such as quoted products, customer contract contents, and so on.

---

[14] The General Data Protection Regulation (EU) 2016/679 (GDPR) is a regulation in EU law on data protection and privacy for all individual citizens of the European Union (EU) and the European Economic Area (EEA).

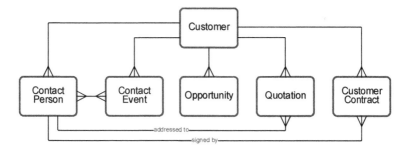

Figure 3-14: Data model describing sample kinds of customer data.

Consequently, the account managers for larger accounts needed to delegate the data content management to others on the account team. Doing that was purely a local decision and completely born out of practical reasons.

According to their enterprise data model, there were many more entities related to the Customer entity, such as the Customer's Invoice and Claim. As that data was not originated close to the account managers, the responsibility for that data resided elsewhere.

In the second data content organization example, the data model did not completely follow the organizational structure. Parts of the product data structure could however be used to address data governance roles, but the data flow and the data life cycle were the key to making data more coherent throughout the organization.

The product line managers were assigned accountability for product data correctness and completeness. The product managers who were reporting to product line managers, were made responsible for all product data concerning their product models throughout the product's entire life cycle. They became product data suppliers, and also product data coordinators, working with their product representatives from other domains, such as pricing, logistics, and aftermarket. All of these people could very well have been called 'operational data workers'.

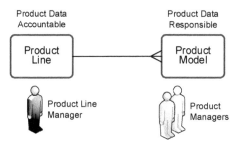

Figure 3-15: Data model detail describing a to-level product structure.

This organization was primarily established to gain efficiency and worked very well. The most important coordination work the product manager did was to follow the product data flow across organizational and geographical borders. The main task for the product line managers, being accountable for product data, was to make sure that this cross-functional data flow was established and in motion.

Business processes completed with master data

The following example describes a situation where a company had data governance for master data and a responsibility structure for managing the business processes. These were organized separately.

There was an early decision taken to let data governance cover nothing more than master data. The idea was to start there, gain experience and then let this knowledge area grow. This scope was prioritized because the master data for products and customers had been a neglected area for ages.

In parallel, work was done to organize responsibility for the business processes. When both data governance and process work were well established and were quite mature, an interesting finding was made; they were incredibly well suited to each other.

The process management work did not pay much attention to master data. It was simply just expected that the data would be available whenever a process was about to be executed. This meant, in turn, that those who worked with master data had well-defined customers for their outcomes. The process management work focused on the data that was used within each process boundary; for example, the invoicing process focused on invoice data, not the master data about customers and sales items. Within the master data work, the master data was centered in terms of covering the entire organization. Within the processes, fast data was of interest, and within master data the static and slow-moving data was the focus.

> *Business process management completed with management of*
> *master data is a very successful marriage.*

Simple enough, the data governance within the process management requires correctness and completeness in order to achieve high process performance, because the customers and the owners required it. The achievement of having high correctness of master data was there because the processes required it. One thing that made this marriage successful was the process managers habit of inviting proper master data entity managers when remodeling the business processes.

Making decisions about data

As a principle of data diplomacy, no new forums or decision-makers are to be organized just because data governance is established. As the responsibility structure for data should follow the existing organizational structure, existing decision forums can be used in most cases.

Figure 3-16: Three vice presidents managing region sales, also being data accountable within each region.

Let us continue with the customer data accountability example in the previous section. The top sales managers, on a vice president level, became data content accountable. In fact, they already had that accountability, as they are accountable for the co-workers in their regions who were acquiring accurate data and making that data available for those who need it. Nobody looked at the organization targeting certain managers to be appointed as data accountable.

Instead, each manager at a certain level such as vice presidents was approached by a data governance lead to clarify "What data are you accountable for?"

They already had VP Sales meetings every second week where data matters could be resolved, if needed. Decisions or statements, in this example, include:

- Comment on changes proposed in the Business Data Design arena.
- Decisions and harmonization regarding rollouts of data design changes.
- Decisions regarding compliance with regulatory requirements affecting data.
- Decisions on accessibility and dissemination of data.
- Addressing data design change requests to the Business Data Design arena (which in practice means taking part

in the design process at the appropriate time and to the appropriate level).

Many of the data decisions made and data improvement actions taken in these meetings happened even before data governance was established. The main difference is that data matters received more attention. Also, that data change matters became directed to the Business Data Design arena. Some of the operational data workers and those who are data accountable are preferably included in the business data design work.

> "Data content management at my job works a little like lubrication in our production. It is silent if everything works but it will crack and squeak if something is wrong."
>
> *Johan Lindholm, data governance lead at a utility company.*

Organizing the Data Processing arena

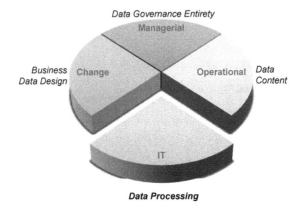

Data Processing

The data governance, business data design, and data content roles meet in the Data Processing arena. The entity managers act as subject matter experts in various projects, either as active parts in the work or though project steering committees.

Business domain data architects communicate the business data design models and guide solution architects and business analysts where to find the model documentation that they need.

The data governance lead and the enterprise data architect are engaged in IT planning to secure the data change aspects in roadmaps and project portfolios. They also work to improve the IT processes to make business data improvement a natural part of the IT work.

All these roles should be prepared to spend time on training and coaching. There are constantly new project members that need to become familiar with the processes that support good data design.

Putting the "I" into IT

The following sections contain suggestions for improvements in common IT activities and processes.

Plugging business data activities into IT processes where data governance roles cooperate is diplomatic. Plugging in gates to check other people's results is coercive.

The "I" in IT stands for "information". Information is concretized by data. The activities described below put the "I" back into the IT, in case anyone had forgotten what IT is all about.

There are a few obvious reasons for including business data-centric activities into IT work:

1. To benefit from the business data design that has already been done, have it translated and developed into system requirements, which can become the system capabilities that the business needs.

2. To ensure that previous data design work is reused, and others can reuse what you find.

3. To create opportunities to achieve shared, consistent and comparable data in ongoing system work.

The suggested data-centric activities are put early in the common IT processes. It is the job of the data governance lead to integrate these activities into these processes. And it is the job of the CIO to sponsor this kind of change.

Project portfolio planning

IT works take budgeting, regardless of who is paying. Portfolio planning is usually an optimization of, or even a trade-off, between funding, business demands, enterprise architecture roadmaps and data improvement strategy. Project portfolios are often prepared by portfolio managers and decided by a CIO.

Using a diplomatic approach, the data governance lead has an agenda of what data will be improved, and the enterprise architect has an idea of what systems should manage what and be transferred where. The enterprise data architect strives for a "normalized" entirety and meaning, aiming for reducing redundant data and promoting data reuse.

If these roles agree on a common picture, they can schedule business data improvement initiatives into projects and activities.

Being two and well prepared increases the chance getting the data design schedule integrated into the project portfolio intact.

It is of great importance to address business data design activities into initiatives and projects. Not only to secure the room for business data design, but also to plan and secure the critical resources for the initiatives and projects. This may need the data governance lead to act.

Modeling business capabilities is a common way for enterprise architects to organize system landscapes and to form and scope projects in roadmaps and portfolio planning. These business capabilities usually just appear in enterprise architects' minds, sometimes in a miraculous way. There is however a methodology to identify and model business capabilities in a data-driven way, described in *Enterprise Architecture Made Simple: Using the Ready Set Go Approach to Achieving Information Centricity*[15]. When the business data is accurately represented in high-level data models, it can be used to influence systems planning and portfolio management.

Project initiation

The data governance lead needs to set the activities for business data modeling in important projects prior to the project's start. Otherwise, the project manager must be convinced to bring such activities into the project plan – which can be a problem as a project manager is eager to exclude everything that is not a part of the expected project delivery. What's more, a business data model is usually not a project deliverable, whereas the system is.

Lastly, when introducing prerequisites for a project and communicating how projects are run, the business design and various data governance activities must be settled in the project plan. Once a project has started it is usually too late. Again, getting it right from the start helps for a smooth delivery.

---

[15] *Enterprise Architecture Made Simple: Using the Ready Set Go Approach to Achieving Information Centricity*, Edvinsson & Aderinne, Technics Publications 2013.

Concept and feasibility studies

As mentioned earlier, the business data design is best performed in the early phases of an IT project. Perhaps, it is even carried out prior to the formal project start. While modeling, reuse existing business data model material; for example, models that are approved and checked into data governance model management, and models that have turned up in parallel initiatives. The whole purpose with this is to move forward in a common direction, and to progress at a common pace, when needed.

Project coordination is expensive and takes time. Coordinating verbally between people is probably the most expensive way of doing it. What is at the forefront of people's minds and the risks being considered are usually topics easily spoken about. But if team members look at each other's data models and sample data, risky overlaps, gaps or confusing representations become immediately obvious.

So, what is it that makes data models and data examples particularly capable to be coordinated? Simply that they reflect easily what a system will handle. If a system does something without any business data being involved, then it is probably not very important.

Data architects usually undertake such coordination work, and by doing that, they become busy bottlenecks. It is therefore better to put entity managers to work by letting them use their networks to coordinate on data matters.

A great way to minimize time-consuming coordination is to hold business data models in workshops, having the interested parties in the same room. Read about conducting business data modeling in workshops in Chapter 4.

Requirement work

During requirement work the business data models are more detailed. This can be done in a project requirement phase or in a sprint. There is a section in Chapter 4 which describes how to detail a business data model based on requirements.

A detailed business data model needs to be aligned with the approved business data models. Being diplomatic, this is done simultaneously as a business design data model is being detailed. This can lead to changing existing data structures which in turn lead to change requests toward approved, or existing, data models. If the appropriate entity manager is included directly, the change request process can be settled in a few hours. Minor changes can even be set by a small email conversation. Keep these things lean.

Somewhere during the detail requirement work, a solution data architect takes over the responsibility of improving the business data, from a business-oriented data architect. It may be the same person having two roles, but this is not preferable.

The business data modeler is an interpreter, a facilitator and the business' advocate. The solution data architect is a systems designer in the IT community. These are two different jobs that require different personalities.

The business data modeler and the systems designer are not enemies.
They are a dynamic duo.

In-house built systems

When building a system, or in another way taking responsibility for the design, it is necessary to verify whether the data design solution meets business expectations, as described in the business data model. This is especially important when the system is used to manage data that is crucial for the business, such as data affecting the customer's perception of value, or data needed to meet regulatory requirements. This can be done by merely comparing the data storage solution with the business data design model. As mentioned previously, a solution data design does not need to be equivalent to a business data design; it just needs to be able to handle the business data.

In the best of all worlds, this check-up should not be needed. However, solution architects bring many other perspectives into the solution data architecture, and when doing that, the business data design is transformed to fit what is about to be built. It is very often about improvements, and those just need a quick check. But, of course, there is always a risk that something might be missed in the transformation.

The heaviest reason for checking a solution design is that a solution architect typically has a project and system perspective, not an enterprise entirety perspective.

The most secure way of mapping business and solution data models is to use example data. Just looking at mock-ups won't give the answer.

The business data design model can be based on designing generic system interfaces, such as Application Programming Interfaces (APIs) in hubs and standardized integration formats. Letting these be influenced by the business data design is a way of distributing the data structure and vocabulary.

Systems acquisitions

Acquiring a commercial off the shelf (COTS) application represents challenges similar to reusing an existing system, such as a solution from a company within the group has built, a group standard application, or what an authority imposes. In these cases, there is really no need for a detailed breakdown of requirements. Similarly, there is no need for an exhaustive requirement data model, detailed as if it would be the basis for implementation. The business data model would most likely do and should provide enough information to determine the implications of using such a system, as it reveals the data structure and the vocabulary. The way to go is the same as checking a solution design in the section above.

It is amazing how many organizations choose to incorporate a system without first checking if it has a data structure that fits.

Pre-launch work

Sometimes, data migration surprises come as a cold shower at the end of IT projects. When this happens, it is an indication of something having been neglected, for instance the consequences of existing data from a developed data structure. Or, the project has not recognized the low quality of the data, something which is possible to assess prior to the project. The quality shortage may even have contributed to the running of the project. The concerned entity manager or the data content accountable should have been connected to the project in some way and have reported the status of the quality.

A part of the diplomatic approach is to be frank about how things really are and trust people to take necessary action.

At some point prior to a system launch, the business data design model turns from a "to be" state to "as-is" state, or rather, "as became". That might include a formal data governance decision. There are those who make decisions on a "to be" business data model, for setting a new standard for a data structure. Others wait until implementation to decide whether a model is valid. If others depend on an approved structure, they need to wait, which could slow them down. But, then again, if a model decision is taken too early, it may change when implemented, and those who are depending on it will need to adapt as well.

Maintenance work

The diplomatic approach to systems maintenance entails simply being awake and aware of coming business data design changes. That means keeping track of what design activities go on and how these could affect future change requests. Sometimes this involves the entity manager and the domain business data architect. An IT maintenance incident may include a quick visit in the Business Data Design arena, and, even in the Data Content arena, if the change implies modifications in data values.

CHAPTER 4

The diplomat's toolbox

The previous chapters have elaborated on the four data governance arenas. This toolbox chapter deals with a few usable tools applicable in any arena.

Initiating data governance in a diplomatic way

The four data governance arenas can, as mentioned earlier, be established and instituted separately and in any order. You can start with one and begin to get some benefits from that.

But let us picture a scenario when starting data governance from a blank paper. What could be a diplomatic and non-coercive way of starting up data governance aiming to produce it formally? Again, it is not rocket science, nor violin playing (which is considered as one of the most difficult instruments to master).

> *If you try to do something you never did before, you simply need to try, learn and go from there.*

It is a little strange that very many choose to start with the formal data governance organization and after that produce some results. Why try to organize something that does not yet exist? That is usually referred to as "big design upstream" and is based on guesses. It will not fly.

It is far better to start working and come up with some experience and some results, and after that, establish the formalities around the work you started doing and the results based on what you have learned. Then you do not guess.

"Lay the eggs before you cackle."[16]

Birgit Nilsson, a humble opera diva

You want to be successful as soon as possible. Therefore, pick the area carefully. If you are (the future) data governance lead, you should be able to select the field. Preferably choose an area in which you have some experience. Do the groundwork by understanding where the most important business data problems are, how they appear to stakeholders, and what their root causes may be. These kinds of problems may have been around a long time, maybe for decades, and people may have involuntary become used to them. Pick a few people who have experienced these problems, have ideas, and are willing to improve them.

---

[16] La Nilsson: My Life in Opera. Northeastern University Press, 2007.

Only work with those who want to make things better.

A mistake many organizations make is that they hire new people to fix enterprise-wide data problems while everybody else keeps on doing what they have always done. Sometimes an armada of consultants is hired to cleanse data and bring in useful technology. What they won't do is to take on the improvement mindset and recognize the normal behavior that cause the problems in the first place. Instead, they allow these behaviors to continue. Such invasion is perhaps suitable and beneficial occasionally. But if armadas of hired data fixers are needed repeatedly, there is need for change in something more fundamental. Just as if you need to see a doctor every month, you might consider making a change in your lifestyle.

Gather "the Knowledgeable individuals"

Take on any role connected with data governance where you think that you can contribute. At the beginning, you may act both as a data governance lead, fragmentary at least, and an enterprise data architect, at least to some extent. Or, you may be interested in the data within the scope you have chosen. Set up a few meetings and mini-workshops with the people you have selected. Just a few hours each will do initially. If they are the people you should have, they can probably spare you these hours as they are eager to stop time-wasting. You might encounter a problem getting access to those who have a coercive, non-diplomatic, manager devoted to spending and time reports; then you will need a sponsor to gain access to them, or, omit them for now.

For anyone asking, "What is my role in this?" the answer is "For now, to contribute with your knowledge. When we know more, we will form a solution and your role as a part of the change will probably be obvious."

At this stage, it is too early to talk roles. If you want to organize something, you will need, as a start, a pile of "something" to organize. That is, it is meaningless to appoint accountability and responsibility for something you do not yet have.

Reveal the situation

The classical situation to start with is a "why". In order to build a community of people who can work together, make a good beginning. Ensure people within the group understand why there is a need for change. Make sure that this awareness is based on facts and that it concerns specific challenges. It can for instance be about obstacles, waste, mistakes, or other phenomena that are or not in line with the organization's goals.

Motivating data governance as a solution for a lack in data quality is as sexy as offering tooth floss.

Initiating data governance solely as a solution, without defining the problems it is intended to solve and without addressing what is to be fixed, is fragile; it can easily be put aside because it is not regarded as a problem, or, there are alternate solutions. Therefore, the path to a lasting change must begin with facts that shed light on how things really are. Only then will the discussion of solutions be meaningful.

The truth is in the data.

Walking through the obstructive data within the scope you have selected will create facts. Having hard figures by transforming the sensed quality shortcomings and obstacles into facts will open people's eyes. Here are a set of fact suggestions:

- Estimate the number of errors in a core register, by checking records with inaccurate data, duplicated records, records containing sparsely-populated data, and format violations. Try to estimate the impacts on the workload efficiency and whether any external error, such as wrong deliveries, could occur from these errors.

- Inspect the amount of correspondence of similar data between two systems and express it in percentage.

- Walk through the systems and documents that contain similar kinds of data within your scope and make a collage of the variations in terminology, data structures, data formats, and data rules. Try to estimate the business consequences of the revealed disparity.

- Draw a data flow depicting the manual steps where data within the scope is transferred between systems and Excel files on a regular basis. Estimate the time spent in manual work and the risk for manual errors in such flow.

- Depict how similar kinds of data are entered and reused by forming a CRUD (create, read, update, and delete) matrix with the type of data on one axis and the systems on the other. To simplify things, skip the "UD" and just point out where data is created and reused. Include in the matrix every system that contains the data in your scope. Draw conclusions of what the matrix reveals. For instance, what the number of duplicate origins of the same data imply for your customers and business partners.

- Brainstorm the benefits and the opportunities by eliminating these data obstacles.

End the study with asking the participants: "How can we prevent things from getting worse, and how can we start moving in the right direction?"

When in a hole, stop digging.

Start making results

Make an effort to fix the problems. You might come up with a study result, such as:

- Recommendation to organize responsibility for quality of the data. Integrate that work in the daily work as a change management task.

- Recommendation to consolidate the data that is managed independently in separate systems.

- A draft business data model depicting how the data really is organized.

- A list of actions that need to be taken.

At this stage the result is purely documentation, ideas and diagrams. No actual change has happened yet. But it is a start.

Be the change

Start acting by doing what is needed. That will, in fact, be how you expect others to act to improve the data. This could include, in relation to the ideas described above:

- "Go to genba"[17]. Be around where the action is, ask questions and look for yourself and discuss the importance of the business data. Discuss what prerequisites are needed for accomplishing the task.

- Contact those who are in charge of the systems concerned, typically a solution manager with a budget for systems maintenance, or similar. Tell them about the work outcome and simply ask what it would take to make the fixes become reality. Try to get an estimate of the efforts.

- Talk to those data architects who work with systems design and also to a few project leaders. If you have an enterprise architect, include that person too. Identify crucial activities that would prevent this kind of situation from happening and would assure continuous data improvements in the future. There is usually a project governance model; a methodology applied where these or an applied development practice of these activities can be allocated.

At this stage the movement has started. A set of important influencers has grabbed your attention and you have gained

---

[17] A Japanese term meaning "the actual place". It can be any "site" such as a construction site, sales floor or where the service provider interacts directly with the customer (Wikipedia).

awareness of something everybody agrees should be improved with ideas and diagrams. Most of these activities can probably be done in a few weeks, without a budget and kept under the managerial radar.

"Making history never starts with asking for permission."

(Anonymous)

At least some managers are informed, possible a few first line managers. And, as the driver of this, you probably have some kind of assignment in order to continue from here. Maybe, it is your first month on the job as a data governance lead. Or, maybe you are just filling a gap and simply doing what needs to be done, like Matt did in his story described in the introduction section.

Start some more tracks like this, preferably in the same neighborhood as it would mean taking advantage of the ripples. Try new areas, be curious and of service. There are companies that continue with the service, and, over the years, they have been getting value from it and slowly this has changed the culture. However, it requires continuity in who runs data governance as well as continuity at the managerial level.

Setting up formal data governance

At a point, the data governance work will need to become organized, and an introductory effort is usually required, and run as a project. Such initiation projects include defining the data governance setup, planning the initial activities and executing these activities. And, as you already have started, much of the groundwork is already done.

An initiation project can for instance result in a formal framework based on the four data governance arenas. A way to do this is to perform the suggested activities in a few projects to test the ambition levels and make these theories and hints become more concrete.

When growing and finding what is working or not, considerations include:

- Is this working, or, do we need some more power? Do we need involvement from a senior manager?

- Are people really engaging in this, or do they just nod and go on as usual?

- Do we need to be more formal in any area? Or, can we release the leash somewhere? Should we delegate and withdraw our engagement and just have a check once in a while?

- Do we have the right level of formalism? Is this a "just enough" level? Formalism can guide but formalism can also prevent or slow down the power of creativity.

Once started and established it may be extended; remember one size cannot fit all. Data governance will target different subcultures, professions, countries and levels in the organizations. Consequently, this must be set up so that it fits various parts of the organization.

Don't expect that your successful data governance set up can be duplicated; it will undergo metamorphoses each time it encounters new targets.

When things are up and running you will notice the following:

- People you engaged to take on this quest are beginning to influence other people's behavior and mindsets. That means that this is getting bigger than you.

- That means that you will need to let go of your control of things. You will need to trust people and delegate. Let them take on their missions and work on with the results they come up with.

You will move from trying to make things happen to becoming a trainer and a coach. You will enter into the entirety tasks that are typical for the data governance lead role. That means letting go of the details and instead focusing on continuing to put business data on everybody's agenda.

Let go when it takes off. Trust people.

Or, you will start all over again in another area and hand over the data governance lead role to someone who is an organizer, rather than an internal entrepreneur. Or you will leave the company and seek new grounds as a data diplomacy missionary.

Diplomacy in action

Capturing business data modeling with business representatives and making them take ownership of the results has been the main focus throughout the book. This tools section is about how it is done in practice; the handcraft of the business data modeling facilitator. It includes a suggested process for the entire work, example agenda for the workshop and a set of hints and considerations for the facilitator. This is the ultimate stage for the data diplomat to run his or her game.

Organizing a business data modeling workshop

When there is uncertainty about the value of the data, what the data means, the designation and how it simply looks, data modeling workshops are an excellent means to settle such matters. However, be careful when considering whether the workshop method is appropriate; run them only when there is a genuine need for it, and, a clear recipient for the results. If these conditions are not met, do not start this process; there must be gravity and a thirst for the outcomes to make people prioritize attendance.

The workshop situation works best when there are different perceptions, such as different opinions between departments, professions and geographical locations. By putting these people with different perspectives in the same room, you create the opportunity, using diplomatic skills, to quickly take big steps forward.

Usually overcoming obstacles in an organization is just about learning and mutually coming to understanding on differences that are largely cosmetic. But sometimes there are large obstacles or permanent stumbling blocks that date back to past experiences. Sometimes there are simply personal differences.

The testimonies in the introductory chapter found elements of sincerity, understanding and trust as a basis for creating lasting change. During a single workshop there is no time to achieve that, especially if the ditches are deep. Here instead factuality that can prevail.

The trick is that the facilitator moves the discussion to data modeling, where the facilitator's knowledge has sovereignty over the combatants. Only then, the facilitator can keep the discussions on neutral ground.

However, it is not appropriate to sell this as a conflict resolution meeting; it is rather a meeting that produces long-awaited and desired results. The entire arrangement must be objectively arranged. It may not even have been an open conflict, and if it were, there is no need to trigger disputes during a workshop. Therefore, contributions for working out an important result should always be invited. In a flattering way, an emphasis can be put on the fact that the best people have been selected based on their knowledge, opinions and foresight.

The person who needs the model result, or his or her client, sets the scope. Most likely, the need for the workshop can be associated with a project, or at least a feasibility study, in favor of the result.

The participant mix is crucial. If it is too narrow a representation, the reliability and confidence in the result will suffer.

"Who participated in this?" is a very common question when suggesting a data design proposal, especially in controversial issues.

The requirements for staffing are as described in the Business Data Design arena in previous chapters; those who have first-hand knowledge of the area, those who have expectations of the business, and those who are directly dependent on the data to be modeled.

The diplomatic facilitator's preparations

Even the most experienced facilitator must set aside time to prepare for a business data modeling workshop. The facilitator will be the "marker holder", i.e. the only one with a whiteboard marker, and will probably be the one who stands up the most. It makes this a scenic situation with the facilitator as an actor in a dramatic play.

Preparations include both reviewing model content and being prepared personally for the work of listening and asking questions. The model content can be prepared with the model's client by doing some sort of shadow modeling before. In this way, the facilitator knows what kinds of areas may emerge and thereby realizes in what order they are to be modeled. In addition, it allows the facilitator to plan the layout of the model thus knowing where to place the first sticker. That reduces the classical "first sticker anxiety". Once the first sticker is nailed, the play has started.

Other preparations include looking in a repository, or in a library of existing models, to understand which entities can be reused in the model to be built. If these entities are defined, and even better, if they are approved, they will save workshop time, in particular if they are peripheral to the coming model. If they are at the center of the model, they may very well be questioned. This is also part of diplomacy; to honor the previously made decisions, and to improve them.

The personal preparation affects the modeling execution. It is about being physically well prepared, as a workshop requires full concentration for several hours at a time. Some workshops last for a couple of days. This means getting a good night's sleep and an early morning so that the facilitator is arrives in time at the venue without stress. Perhaps arriving an hour prior to the workshop, having coffee and having had a small talk with the project manager or the project's client facilitates a calmer procedure.

Professional facilitators always made sure that every marker works, all material for the workshop is available, the computer is charged, and, the projector and communication technology works. The facilitator is well-rested, inspired and in a good mood. That way, she or he is well equipped for a demanding task without being disturbed by avoidable obstacles. Should conflicts arise, aggressions spill over onto the facilitator as well. If you are not in good shape, it is easy to lose your temper, which you cannot as then you are no longer diplomatic.

Workshop execution

A workshop is like a play, or a concert, with the participants as actors, or players, and the facilitator as the director, or the conductor. This means that the artwork cannot start with the heaviest part. Concerts and plays usually reach a climax after an hour, or so. The opening can of course be impressive, and also massive, but you will not get a response for a while until the participants are confident of what this is all about. If you expect a roar from an audience when entering a stage as a data modeler, you do not have proper expectations about your profession. Rather, you will gain respect by earning it, starting at zero in every workshop.

A successful workshop contains the following steps.

1. **Introduction to the task.** That includes a personal presentation and a description of the intended outcome of the workshop, the expectations of what it will contribute to, and who the customer is for the workshop results.

2. **Introduction to the methodology.** As there will be mainly business representatives present, they will need a short introduction to business data modeling syntax, enough to understand what it expresses. A simple explanation of what an entity is and what cardinality means is usually enough. Invest ten or fifteen minutes in doing this well.

3. **Identifying the entities.** After the introductions, which may take three quarters of an hour, the next "investment" in time is to collect the model material. Even if you are well prepared, ask questions about what they want included in the model. If there is an issue to

resolve, someone could reveal the situation by showing truthful data. The result from this step is a list of concepts to be modeled. It not to be an exhaustive list, just enough to get started.

4. **Modeling in pieces.** From there, it is just modeling. Select a few entities at a time and model them. Be sure to keep focused on these entities and work through them one by one. Settle the definition of an entity and put that into the model. After that, settle a related entity and establish the relationship line and its cardinalities. Determine if that entity has relationships to any of the entities that have been modeled so far. Never introduce an entity that cannot be related to those which are settled. Save it until there is something to relate it to.

Building a data model in a workshop is somewhat similar to putting up a tent. If a participant has never seen the tent up, he or she has just an idea of how it will appear. Nobody else has a similar picture. What you do as a facilitator is to find level ground, place the fabrics and find a spot to raise the first pillar. That is layout and model planning. The first physical step is when you hammer in the first two or three pegs. In business data modeling situations, this is to determine the first two or three entities and connect them with labeled relationships. After eight to twelve pegs, the participants can see the tent go up and understand what it is about. This may take a few hours but when it happens it is the peak of the artwork. The tempo will accelerate and you, the facilitator, will turn from asking for material to the model into controlling the eagerness to complete the model. Do not rush at this point. Just continue to follow the methodology in steps. You will earn respect from that.

When the modeling is done, meaning, that the model receiver is happy with it, it is time to document the result. Sometimes one workshop is enough. Sometimes it will take a series of meetings to complete it, including other participates to fill in their opinions and insights.

In many cases documenting is just to use a drawing tool for the diagrams, a spreadsheet for the data examples, a word processor for the definitions. But if the modeling has resulted in something controversial or something entirely new, it is worth spending time to document the model as a "model story". That is explained in a section below.

Data modeling workshop pitfalls

I know a modeler who can produce excellent models. He has designed many data models that he has written books with generic models that are ready to use. However, the way he makes models leaves a great deal to be desired.

He asks questions and starts thinking. After a while his mind has created something, and he starts drawing it and selling his idea to the others. While doing so he realizes a problem, a shortcoming, a missing piece, and corrects himself. So, while presenting his data model design, he is arguing with himself, back and forth, correcting his model, which results in a smudgy sketch.

"This is it. Look! It must be one-to-many over here, right?" he says with his back facing everybody.

He goes over his design, constantly looking at his artwork, reading aloud what the model says, not what it implies. He turns to his audience, expecting gratitude for his brilliance. The birdhouse[18] look on their faces is, however, not a result of admiration. It is one of being completely lost.

"It does it, right? Maybe you don't get it, yet."

He has made all the diplomatic mistakes.

- He would have produced a model that would be better understood if he had included others in the process of designing it.

- He would then have got it right from start.

- He would have thus been ready earlier.

---

[18] "A birdhouse look on one's face" is an old Swedish expression of someone sitting with an open mouth, either of being astonished, or lost.

- He would also have had the model accepted.

- He would have saved many hours after the session since he would not have needed to constantly guard his own outcome.

What a diplomatic data modeling facilitator should do is to save the model idea silently, as a private tacit knowledge. Instead of invading everybody with an idea, believing that this idea is better than everybody else's, the facilitator should ask questions that will verify the design validity.

Here is another case; a well-experienced data architect tried to facilitate a group of subject matter experts to capture their data requirements for a new system. When done, he encountered a problem.

> "I put my soul into this business data model. It took me months to get ready. But the implementation guys didn't use it. They started all over on a blank paper."

> *An experienced business data architect.*

My response was as follows. If you put so much of *your* soul into it, it will become too close to *you*. Nobody else has understood it and they have probably logged out long before you were satisfied with it. My advice would be to lower your expectation of completeness and instead, adapt to their opinions on completeness. You have an amount of time with a set of business representatives. Worship that time and model what they need in order to express the core elements that fixes the problem their project is facing. And, again, make it *their* model instead of yours. Then they will make sure that it is used.

"The best is the enemy of the good."

Françoise Voltaire

Diplomatic workshop hints

Use a business-friendly data modeling syntax such as the one described in the Data Design arena in previous chapters. Have a few colors on stickers for distinguishing stickers that are entities, a few attributes or data examples. Always enrich the model with attributes and examples as it explains the model well.

Do not use the UML (Unified Modeling Language) when modeling business data with business representatives. It goes without saying, but for those who question this there are academic studies revealing the shortcomings on the UML readability[19].

Avoid doing data design modeling using a computer. Use a whiteboard, stickers and markers when modeling. Use a high-resolution camera to include any remote participants. Having

---

[19] *Evaluating the Visual Syntax of UML: An Analysis of the Cognitive Effectiveness of the UML Family of Diagrams.* Daniel Moody and Jos Hillegersberg, Springer-Verlag Berlin, 2009.

remote participants can work ok when presenting and verifying a model, but can be hard to engage them when doing a creative data design. They are easily in the back seat in such process.

The diplomatic data modeling facilitator should ask questions until those answers appear that contribute to the growth of the model. And when good answers come, the people who made the model grow will feel rewarded. Such a reward is, of course, small, but the other participants quickly realize what it is all about. If you are to have a chance to influence the data model design, then it is necessary to provide answers that make the design progress.

In diplomacy you use how human nature works. If there is a reward in contributing, then interest will grow.

Data modeling workshops can be very talkative. Listening to all the dialog can be challenging. Here are a few listening hints:

- Those who are the most talkative are not necessarily right.

- Those who are silent may have something to say.

- HIPO (HIghest Paid Opinion) is not the truth, but probably excellent guidance for design directions. And, their presence increases the confidentiality in the results.

- The most secure and self-confident ones are not necessarily those who know the best.

- Those who are suspicious and careful may just be frightened.

- Those who are suspicious and careful might be right.

The entity definitions, the relationship cardinalities, and entity naming, should be determined solely by asking questions. In this way, a model is put together with a sense of ownership for the result. The worst thing you can do as a facilitator is to question their results. The word "facilitating" actually means "making it easy to reach what you are after".

A skilled facilitator makes hard things appear easy.

This is not equivalent to simplifying the results, i.e. discarding complexity. There might be complex structures that need to be resolved and redesigned. Making such a task easier is about processing it in a structured way, by distinguishing known from unknown complex structures, and, "raising the tent" in steps and thereby isolating the difficult complexities from the manageable ones.

Let the representatives introduce others, such as new participants, to the model work. An accepted and well-understood model is best presented by business representatives themselves. They are more in number and this means that the business data design is more widely distributed. They are also much more credible when it comes to explaining the purpose of the model's proposed changes. Moreover, they are much better at handling any objections to the model design.

Ask instead of tell. The only occasion a neutral facilitator speaks up is when presenting existing models from previous adjacent modeling.

As a facilitator, you need to avoid AtBR: Addicted to Being Right. Let other people win. If you need to win you are not diplomatic. The enterprise's benefits from you being right is not that big; that it is more about yourself. Furthermore, if you "win" you will also win the ownership of the result.

Do have intense discussions. That is just energy. Nobody remembers lame meetings. On the contrary, results that have taken effort are something that people remember with a smile and are proud of.

A business data model is a document that expresses requirements regarding business data. The process of producing it is however something else; it is also a business development process. We question and agree on data structures and terminology. While doing that we undergo a process of understanding different perspectives and viewpoints, and, trying to find a path of moving forward as a company. During such data design, we are probably not thinking of the responsibilities of a single department or remaining in the scope of a certain project. When being creative we need freedom, not obstacles.

The outcome of such process is understanding and communication. In fact, there are occasions where a business data modeling session only ends up with insights; not any useful diagrams at all for IT professionals to dig into. This is an example where the working process and the debate is more important than the actual result. The result may very well stay with insights that lead to actions that cleanse the vocabulary and ease the internal communication. Most communication between humans is still not digital.

Fact-based business requirements

This section is about using a business data model as a diplomat's tool for formulating requirements for IT systems.

Being neutral is an act of diplomacy and basing decisions underpinned by indisputable facts is a way to stay neutral. Selecting an IT-system is a decision that is seldom regarded as a neutral act. Conversations like this can be heard in connection with system selections:

"This is the best system on the market. It meets our requirements."

"There are better systems. The requirements must have been biased toward your assumed favorite system."

Requirements for an IT-system should not be a wish list, nor just a list of disappointments with existing system. They must be stricter than that.

An IT requirement is a necessary capability, or a constraint, addressed toward technology. It is motivated by, and thereby derived from, an expectation of the organization.

Identifying and formulating business requirements on IT is a challenge. Among the challenges are:

1. capturing the essential requirements and not only today's shortcomings (or biases toward a known system),

2. writing verifiable requirements (enabling them to be checked to see if they are fulfilled),

3. writing understandable requirements (understandable enough to validate whether any requirement is an accurate description of what is actually needed),

4. avoiding overlaps and gaps in requirements, and

5. avoiding contradictions in a large stack of requirements (which is hard when not having a proper requirement structure).

As if a business-owned data model is a miracle substance that can cure anything, it can actually resolve these five challenges to some extent, enough to make it worth using it in requirement management.

Advantages

A business data model covers business requirements related to data.

A business data model expresses requirements on the capability of a system's design without stipulating the design of the system.

It expresses what kind of data the system should be able to store and process, and, how that data should be structured and connected. It can also express requirements on vocabulary. It does not cover how data should be processed and transferred; that takes other kinds of requirements. Still, there are a set of advantages for just having it. Here are a few:

- A data model is graphical and enables people to see whether any details might be missing. A model diagram is easier to read than lots of text.

- It is possible to check the data model against a system to see if all the data requirements are fulfilled.

- It is normalized, that is, one thing occurs just once, so nothing is overlapped. As the entities are related in a data model, we do not have gaps.

- A data model expresses some of the business rules. All other business rules use data in at least some way. Rules are fed with data.

- Using a data model as a table of contents for requirements, e.g. a requirements structure, for functions, rules and restrictions on data, helps avoid contradictions in requirements.

Let's show this in an example.

Figure 4-1: Business requirements expressed as a business data model.

There are many requirements expressed in the model in Figure 4-1. It is a perfect starting point for a business analyst or a requirement expert to start analyzing requirements on how a system should be built. The graphical diagram communicates that the system should/must be able to:

- organize Sales Items into Assortments.

- manage a Sales Item so that it can occur in more than one Assortment.

- keep track of Assortments so that they can be aimed to a Target Group.

These requirements are declared by the model's relationships and thus just translatable. But there are also some hidden demands such as that the system should/must be able to manage:

- Sales Items,
- Assortments and
- Target Groups.

The fact that something is defined as an entity implies that the data the entity represents should be manageable in a system. That means that the data should be uniquely identified, have private attributes, and possibly have CRUD capabilities.

Each entity, each relationship, and each relationship line end is a requirement.

After this, it is a requirement analysis matter to determine what functionality is required. Maybe there is need for CRUD capabilities for some of these entities in the target system. If not, there is most likely an integration requirement if the data is just expected to be there. Furthermore, as an input to data storage design, the data storage structure solving the small model example may appear in many ways. The important thing is that a business user can experience whether a Sales Item has a many-to-many relationship with Assortment or not. That does not mean that the database needs to be designed that way.

A real-world experience

I was hired by the CIO at a real estate and facility management company. She was modernizing the entire technical platform having many systems to acquire, and consequently many projects to coordinate. I was mostly facilitating workshops to form the business process and to design business data as a base for requirements for these projects. We were quite busy doing that. She was great to work with, but planning was not her favorite task.

One Wednesday afternoon the CIO informed me that the vendor for an interesting facility management system was about to visit next Friday morning, two days from then, where they would present their system.

"Ok", I said, "but we have not gathered any requirements in that area yet."

"You're right, we can do that tomorrow afternoon", she replied. "I think we can call in a few people to contribute to the kind of model you are used to drawing."

That was the way this CIO was. Trusting people, but also exposing people to pressure. She wanted to keep up the speed on things. In this case, she also wanted to challenge this vendor's almost provocative suggestion to discuss requirement fulfillment with just a few days' notice. The vendor was probably hoping to have an unprepared client and thereby aiming to take control of the situation, and, getting a profitable contract from that.

For me, this meant having just a three-hour workshop to gather requirements for the entire facility management area. I chose to make a quick business data model with the people I got. We already had the data models from earlier work, depicting the facilities from their physical perspective, and, from a commercial perspective. That meant, we had already modeled what the houses and the equipment looked like and how the spaces were contracted with clients. We "just" needed to add the facility management part of this.

During the workshop we started to resolve two questions:

- What is vital to keep track of within the scope for facility management? A set of concepts was listed.

- What characterizes successful facility management? A draft description of expectations was noted.

Having that, we produced a business data model that Thursday afternoon. Two thirds of the model were simply reused from previous sessions, so we spent most of the time on the parts that were missing. We finished by checking what parts of the model were crucial to fulfill the expectations.

When the vendor arrived the next morning, they saw the model which had been left on the whiteboard from the day before.

After some polite phrases were exchanged, the CIO went up to the model and said:

"These are our prioritized data requirements. Note that we have a quite unique physical facility structure, and, that we have chosen to distinguish the physical from commercial facility structure. Now, let us look into your product and how you would solve that. After that, we are interested in how your system would bring us a successful facility management."

Having just an afternoon to prepare an evaluation of a COTS, I chose to use that time to produce a business data model in order to have something to compare the system against.

What data a system can store sets the limit of the support a system can give the operations.

I focused on the data structure and the entity definitions (by using examples) to get as much as I could. I didn't worry that much about semantics and attributes in such a time range.

The system's vendor representatives realized that this client was definitely leading them, not the other way around, as they had planned. A month later, a deal was made, and the CIO got a good price. It was not the world-class system they could have possibly received, but they knew what they were buying, they knew it fit well into their systems landscape in terms of data, and, they could start fast and began to quickly receive the benefits from it.

Data model storytelling

In the previous section, examples were shown of how a data model can be transformed into requirement text. In this section, we will develop such transformations and look at how a data model can be described as a story. A data model story is a tool for communicating a data model for those who do not know data modeling.

The problem with business data models is that they are perfectly clear to you if you are involved in building them. When they are finished, people who were not present when modeling them, as well as people who were there but no longer remember what they were about, cannot easily read them. However, there is no problem understanding a business data model if the facilitator who led the modeling work presents the model pedagogically. Such a method of communicating knowledge is very slow and depending on the moment so the result is not easy to spread widely. But a document is easier to distribute, and a data model story is simply the facilitator's model presentation written down in text, with data examples and images of the data model added.

A data model story is a business data model explained in text and diagram clips, intended for business and IT representatives to understand the core concepts of a business data design. A data model story uses business vocabulary and does not assume that the readers master data modeling.

Picture a situation where a group of far-sighted experts made a business data design that, if implemented, would present great opportunities. In order for such a thing to become a reality, many people must gain the same insights as those who participated in the design of the data. For example,

- we want to know if we are, at all, thinking properly,

- we want to know if we have missed something,

- we may want to know how bold the approach is that we have taken, and if it is at all possible,

- we want to know how people react to our proposal, or,

- we simply want to explain what we have come up with.

Then, it is worth the effort to write a data model story. A model story can also describe an approved data model and be intended mainly for knowledge sharing. It is then an excellent description for those who are affected by a coming change including a new system. Also, for those who are about to utilize complex data models, such as technical configuration models and production automatization, or very generic data models with vague vocabulary.

There are organizations which have a model story document as a mandatory step prior to a formal data design decision in their data governance process.

Model story contents

Data model storytelling is not new. Back in 2001, Len Silverston released a book with generic data models[20], showing what an enterprise model may look like, and, what a model story can look like. The entire book describes a consistent enterprise data model. Each chapter is a subject area, and, a section in each chapter reflects a detailed model within a subject area. Each entity is introduced, one at the time, having a definition, a few data examples, the most vital attributes and how this relates to previously introduced entities. A model story should include all this and, a couple things about the modeling process and what it is expected to lead to.

Table 4-1 contains an example table of contents for a model story document that describes a design proposal. The headers

---

[20] *The Data Model Resource vol. 1 – a Library of Universal Data Models for All Enterprises*, Len Silverston et al, John Wiley & Sons, 2001.

can be phrased differently as well as the structure of the document, but most of the contents should be there.

Model Story table of contents
Introduction
   Purpose with the model and this story
   Modeling procedure and participants
   Deciding the proposal
The as-is structure
   Part 1
   Part 2
   Part n
   Data examples
   Shortcomings with today's structure
Proposed structure
   Part 1
   Part 2
   Part n
   Data examples
   The entire model proposal
   Fulfilling expectations using this structure
Implementation considerations
How to read a business data model

Table 4-1: Data Model Story table of contents

A model story needs an introduction explaining what challenges the model aims to solve, the driver behind the modeling efforts, and what the continued work consists of. It also needs to be clear what expectations the reader is faced with. The business data design decision process needs to be clarified if the model story describes a proposal.

If data governance is instituted, there is probably a metadata repository, a business glossary or other kind of semantic library available. If so, the data model story needs to relate to the official version of the checked in material in such a library.

Data model proposals need to reveal important changes in a data design, and thereby include both the as-is structure and the proposal. A few revealing data examples are vital. Not only to understand the difference between as-is and suggested to-be, but because the proposal needs to prove that the suggested model fulfills the expectations. Furthermore, the data examples will explain whether the suggested data design implies that new data is needed; data that we do not yet have but which needs to be available in some way.

If the story is not a proposal for decision, but perhaps just a description, only one version is needed; preferably an existing structure, a preferred structure, or, a desired structure.

A data model story should not be limited to describing the data in a single system. Like any business data model, the vocabulary, the structure and the relationships should strive to depict how the business data truthfully appears, regardless, and neutral to, existing systems.

Just remember that even if you explain a business data model in the most popular and amusing way, a model story will still be heavy to digest. Give people time to absorb it.

A data model story example

Below is an example of a data model described as a model story. The example depicts real estate and building structures for university premises proposed as a base for a future master data system. The model is very simplified.

As mentioned earlier, when a one-to-many relationship line has a name, it reads from the many-side. That is, crow's foot side, of the relationship line. The benefit with that rule is shown in the data examples; these relationship names can occur as headers in the example tables, such as the "Construction *located on* Property" in example Table 4-2.

Construction

A Construction is a terrestrial structure that creates a venue for a determined kind of business. A Construction is either a Building or a Facility.

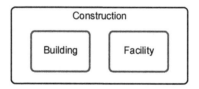

A Building is a house that contains one or more spaces bounded by floors, walls and ceilings. A Facility is a work that is not a house, such as sports grounds, radio and telecommunication masts, bridges, energy plants, or prepared land in connection with a property.

A Building is typed into a Building Purpose, such as education, laboratory or library. Likewise, a Facility is of a Facility Type, for example ground, energy plant, mast, or fountain.

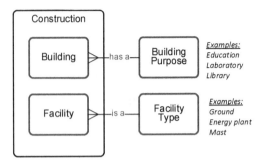

Proposed change: we generalize buildings and facilities to a common concept to enable common maintenance responsibilities.

A Property is an area of a land that is entered in, or to be entered in, an official property registers as an independent legal entity. A Construction is located on a Property.

There can be zero, one or more Constructions (i.e. Buildings or Facilities) on a Property. A Construction normally belongs to a Property, but there are a few exceptions where buildings extend over more than one Property.

Proposed change: we introduce property as a placeholder for constructions. That way, we can separate the physical constructions from ownerships, as we strive to keep track of property owners rather than construction owners.

Below are a few examples of Constructions, covering the data model so far:

Id #	Construction Name	Purpose / type	Year built	located on Property	Subtype
1	Carolina Redeviva	Library	1819	U 1:32	Building
2	Svedberg	Laboratory	1986	E 2:19	Building
3	South heat center	Energy plant	2009	U 1:32	Facility

Table 4-2: Construction examples with attributes and relationships

Construction Section

A Construction Section is a distinguishable part of a Construction, such as a house body, which may be constructed for a certain purpose. A Construction Section can be an expansion of a Construction, built at a later stage than the rest of the building.

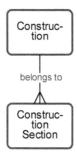

A Construction Section can for instance have separate data that distinguishes attributes of sections from those of the building in general.

Proposed change: we introduce construction sections as a new detail level to manage maintenance, utilities and operations more granularly.

Construction Section	*belongs to* Construction	Year built
The cantina	Carolina Redeviva	1945
Heat exchanger	South heat center	2018

Table 4-3: Construction Section examples

Location Address

A Location Address uniquely indicates a location. There may be multiple addresses to a Building, for example because several streets surround it.

The entire Construction model, as defined so far:

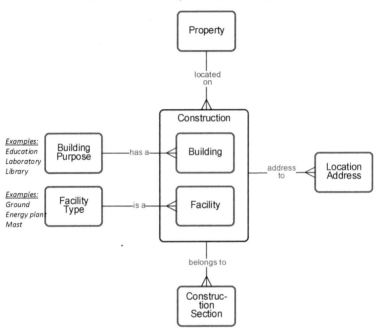

A data model story is not very hard to write if you have assigned a name to all the relationships and phrased a definition of each entity. Then it is just about coming up with an idea which orders the entities and the relationships to be introduced and expressing that idea clearly in words.

Well invested model storytelling efforts

During the first decade of 2000, a colleague and I took on a large modeling assignment. Using the methodologies described in this chapter, we modeled the data covering the global spare part management for a large automotive company. They were about to make a major change to several business processes including the spare part services, logistics, processes and, consequently, the systems. We had a workshop team of experts to lean on who took the task of designing the new spare handling business, and my colleague and I were their interpreters toward a business data model. It took us about three months to capture the business' data requirements. Occasionally we needed to be quite detailed to explain and reveal the core ingredients in their future spare part handling. We ended up with about 250 entities and consequently around 1,000 relationships. While modeling that data structure we managed to capture a brief definition of, or at least the purpose of, each entity and each relationship.

Even though many experts contributed to the work, the data model needed to be validated. Approximately a couple hundred business representatives around the world were expected to express their opinions on it. We knew that just e-mailing a file with diagrams and attaching a definition list would just be intimidating. So, my colleague and I spent two weeks writing a model story, ending up with a 75 pages document that explained the new spare part management data model. We distributed it two weeks before Christmas and asked to have the replies during the second week of January.

Surprisingly, we got feedback from 95% of the respondents who gave us lots of comments on the model. Hardly any one of the respondents had had any experiences from data modeling. None of them had been present in the workshops. Their only input was the model story document. Still, they could understand and improve the model. The weeks writing the story was indeed well invested time.

The five running guys

This last section of the book is about the benefits, and also challenges of including heterogeneity in mindsets whenever facing an important change in the organization.

The earlier chapters describe how different roles and departments need to be represented in the data design process. These people represent different kinds of requirement areas and therefore different perspectives on the data. But, there is another important dimension to this; different ways of thinking need to be represented in a group that undertakes to shape the future. The group cannot be a uniform collection of positivists because then the result will be biased toward success. Nor can it be a group of negativists or scary-cats because then there will be no progress.

Figure 4-2: The five running guys.

A great mix would be a representation of one of each of the five running guys[21]:

- One looking forward
- One looking at the back of the first running guy
- One looking up
- One looking down in the ground
- One looking backward.

Without thinking about it, the earth spins, and we spin with it. Similarly, the organization's environment is changing and the organization changes with it, whether we think about it or not. As explained in the introduction chapter, when there is a change, there is gravity. Therefore, these five guys are depicted as running, because they are affected by the gravity and the movement, whether they notice it or not.

Each of these five guys represents a personal strategy in handling the ongoing changes. Let us have a look at each one of them in more detail.

The first guy from the left is moving forward, not very fast, and looking backward. What lies ahead is guesswork and what has happened is true. The past gives insight for this guy and it guides him with what to do if it happens again. The second guy has a

---

[21] Even if they are referred as "guys" and "him" the story of course also includes "gals" and "her".

full and narrow perception of all the details. This specialist knows where the devil resides and knows how to find him. The third guy is looking upward and keeping track of all the expectations from above, including decisions taken, incentives and direct orders.

Having preconceptions and being prejudiced, these first three guys can correspond to certain stereotypes. This is just for fun, of course (almost):

- The Finance department looks back as it is their job to keep account and report of what has happened. The Legal department also prefers to look back as their world is based on rules that are already written.

- Operations look down as they need to focus on today's matters. The need to see where they put their feet and to focus on that, saving long-term challenges for later.

- C-levels and higher levels of middle management look up as they are trapped in the hierarchy and the "advance-or-go" philosophy. They are occupied to fulfill the expectations from above and to maneuver properly as if in a game of chess. It is not only about doing the job; it is also about keeping it and moving upwards.

It is, of course, possible to have backward-looking reactionists in product development departments, and downward-looking detail fusspots may be found anywhere. And there are of course forward-looking strategists in the Finance department. And most middle managers can look in other directions than up.

Anyway, moving on to the next guy. Let's save the fourth guy for now and move on to the last.

The guy on the far right is forward-looking and has visions of how things will become in the future along with ideas of actions that need to be taken. When running, this guy runs ahead of all the others. The guy on the far right is vital to have onboard for a change process. This is the audacious innovator. Almost every competitive company wishes to a have a bunch of these guys.

The second guy from the right, the one who is looking at the back of the fifth guy, is also vital since the innovator must have someone supporting the bold ideas. A follower encourages the innovator and confirms that the ideas are working, wanted and needed (when they are). It takes courage to be the first follower of a bold idea, so this is a frontrunner without the audacious ideas. This follower will be the innovator's advocate.

However, do not leave these two guys on the right of the diagram alone with a generous budget. They could easily ruin a wealthy business. That is why the other guys are needed in the design process: to make this become more than just a blueprint.

The backward-looking guy represents the past and recalls experiences from similar attempts. Thanks to this guy, a business design can learn from previous mistakes. A runaway stallion needs this person to hold back the reins.

The downward-looking guy represents reality and can include sanity into wild ideas. Thanks to this guy, the business design can be reasonably bold and possible to create, at least in steps.

The upward-looking guy represents the owner's or the executive's expectations and can relate the value of the business design to attract the senior management. Thanks to this guy, the design can be funded.

Having two forward-lookers, the innovator and the follower, is however necessary to balance skepticism. Here is the mathematical proof:

$$1 - 1 = 0$$
$$1 + 1 - 1 = 1$$

Hence, it takes at least two positivists to gain a positive result when dealing with a negativist.

In such a mix of personalities, there will be contradictions. There will probably be strong emotions expressed and possibly some eruptions. But emotions do not kill. Rather, they add strength needed to come out of an exhausting process. And, it is not possible to be passionate about something without putting emotions into it. This is where diplomacy ultimately comes into play. Recognizing different perspectives is the first step to enabling wider perspectives. No matter what result is produced in such a constellation, progress still takes place. Everyone will start looking in other directions:

- The guy who looks back realizes that others are heading somewhere.

- The head of the one looking down gets up and realizes that there are directions that are longer than a single step.

- The one who looks up starts looking around and where to put his feet.

- Those who look ahead begin to realize that more people have to keep up.

Picture a group of business delegates representing each running guy. Imagine the outcome. Then picture a group that is missing one of the guys and what kind of data design they would come up with. Imagine *that* outcome.

Here is a testimony from Mimmi, an experienced business analyst and an excellent data architect. She was obtaining the business requirements to put forward the requirements on how to modernize product data.

"I need to talk to a forward-looking guy, but I can't find that person. My fear is that this design is paving the cowpath. Tomorrow's solution will just be today's business, just without the software problems they experience today."

The five running guys is the last diplomatic hint. For now.

Index

www.ingramcontent.com/pod-product-compliance
Lightning Source LLC
Chambersburg PA
CBHW071240050326
40690CB00011B/2207